CONCILIUM

concilium

1999/5

2000: REALITY AND HOPE

Edited by
Virgil Elizondo and
Jon Sobrino

SCM Press · London
Orbis Books · Maryknoll

Published by SCM Press Ltd, 9–17 St Albans Place, London N1
and by Orbis Books, Maryknoll, NY 10545

Copyright © Stichting Concilium

English translations © 1999 SCM–Canterbury Press Ltd and Orbis Books,
Maryknoll

All rights reserved. No part of this publication may be reproduced, stored in a
retrieval system, or transmitted, in any form or by any means,
electronic, mechanical, photocopying or otherwise,
without the prior written permission of
Stichting Concilium, Prins Bernhardstraat 2 6521 A B Nijmegen, The Netherlands

ISBN: 0 334 03056 0 (UK)
ISBN: 1 57075 229 X (USA)

Typeset at The Spartan Press Ltd, Lymington, Hants
Printed by Biddles Ltd, Guildford and King's Lynn

Concilium Published February, April, June, October, December.

Contents

Editorial   vii
    Virgil Elizondo and Jon Sobrino

I · The Globalizing Evil of Our Actual World   1

Life and Death on Planet Earth   1
    Leonardo Boff

Some Specific Cases   12
    1. The Situation of Africa   12
       Elizabeth Amoah
    2. The Mayas of Chiapas   18
       Carlos Mendoza-Álvarez
    3. 'Death Row' USA   24
       John Mannion

A Carefully Hidden Reality   30
    Enrico Chiavacci

Sins of the World, Light of the World   39
    José-Ignacio González Faus

II · The Hope of the Jubilee in Religious Traditions   51

The Jubilee in Judaeo–Christian Tradition   51
    Elsa Tamez

Jubilee 2000 in the Teaching of John Paul II   59
    David N. Power

Asian Dreams and Christian Hope   66
    Felix Wilfred

A Jubilee in Jeans   75
    Donna Singles

III · Hope and Grace   81

Resurrection: The Ground, Power and Goal of our Hope   81
    Jürgen Moltmann

Sources of Hope   90
   1. The Women's Movement   90
      Maria Pilar Aquino
   2. Ethics   95
      Marciano Vidal
   3. Greater Love, Witness to Full Life   100
      Eduardo de la Serno
   4. Renewing the Face of the Earth   105
      J. Matthew Ashley
A Total Jubilee: 'Giving Hope to the Poor and Receiving It
  from Them'   111
  Jon Sobrino

IV · Closing Reflections   121
Jubilee Litanies   121
  Pedro Casaldáliga

Contributors   125

Editorial

Throughout its history, humankind has rethought its situation, sometimes with the intention of undoing the evil that besets it and 'turning history back', in the words of Ignacio Ellacuria. This supposes an ongoing hope that justice, solidarity and peace are a possibility for the human family. It also supposes the need for conversion. This idea is common to many cultural and religious traditions; it is central in the biblical-Christian tradition, and the idea that hope is from and for the poor is basic to this.

'Jubilee' can well be taken as the term to express this examination of conscience, this hope and this decision to change. In this number of *Concilium* Elsa Tamez analyses its Old Testament connotation, while Felix Wilfred looks at it in Eastern religious traditions. Donna Singles relates it to young people today, and David Power examines it in the theology and pastoral teaching of John Paul II, who has made such extensive use of the term. These are not the only expressions of desire or longing for 'strong times' in history, in which we human beings ask ourselves where we are and where we want to go, but they are enough to show that the Jubilee is an important reality in our day. If we put forward different points of view, it is to learn from one another how to celebrate it in the most efficacious way.

For Jubilee 2000 not to be a docile and easily co-optable event, it has to be celebrated in the real world. We therefore have to try to establish where we are in regard to good and evil, life and death, hope and despair in our world, and above all what resources we have to make this world more human. So, without 'oppressing truth with injustice', but paying due honour to reality, we analyse it as both mystery of salvation and mystery of iniquity.

Dealing with the iniquity, Leonardo Boff examines the globalization of evil in the world. Elizabeth Amoah and C. Mendoza Álvarez expound two raw realities of our time: the continent of Africa and the Mexican region of Chiapas. John Mannion analyses the death penalty and the constellation of evils that surrounds it. E. Chiavacci reveals how the evils of our situation are deliberately covered up. Finally, José Ignacio González Faus provides the historical background and modern application of the deep biblical intuition of the sin of the world.

While we cannot celebrate the Jubilee without being conscious of this situation of sin – and making it central – neither can we celebrate it without taking account of the manifestations of good and of grace in our present-day world, which, often against hope, keep up the hope of the poor. This has its logical priority. So Jürgen Moltmann traces hope and grace systematically back to the resurrection of Jesus. Other articles provide specific examples, old and new, of the workings of good and grace in upholding hope. María Pilar Aquino analyses the women's movement; Marciano Vidal the goodness of heart of simple people; J. Matthew Ashley advances in science and technology. Eduardo de la Serna goes back to the origin of all Christian hope: martyrdom, the greatest love, witness to the fullness of life. Finally, Jon Sobrino looks at the concept of 'total Jubilee' based on the good news of Jesus of Nazareth: the table shared in such a way that not only do the poor take hope from us, but we too take it from them.

The aim of all these articles is to put forward a Christian vision of Jubilee. This is above all for the poor and victims of this world, for the crucified peoples: this is the tradition of Leviticus. But we should like to add something more novel and more scandalously Christian: the salvation the poor bring to their oppressors – the tradition of the Servant of Yahweh – so that the Jubilee works in two directions. This is important if – from a historical perspective – the Jubilee is not to be reduced to aid from the North to the South (which is certainly necessary and in justice has to be given as reparation), but is also understood as aid – in humanization – from the South to the North (which is perhaps even more urgent and necessary and is certainly what will make this world change).

Seen in this way, celebration of the Jubilee supposes recognition of a most serious conflict in our world, along with hope for conversion. Being a Christian Jubilee, it also supposes announcing the good news of Jesus Christ to the poor, with the hope that this Jesus will change hearts of stone into hearts of flesh. The ultimate hope is that the good news of Jesus will continue to be a real possibility today and that Christians of all denominations, believers of all religions, and all human beings of good will may communicate it today and help to make this world a shared table.

The celebration of the Jubilee has, then, nothing to do with Western church triumphalisms, nor with unreal messianisms, nor with folkloric escapisms. It does not take us away from the harsh reality of our world. But, as humans and as Christians, neither can we pass over the question of whether 'there is something good in history to celebrate', still less whether today, in spite of everything, justice is truer and stronger than oppression, hope than despair, life than death. Our answer involves the core of the Christian faith. This is what Pedro Casaldáliga has expressed in the form of prayer in his 'Jubilee Litanies', which begin with these words:

God of Love, our Father, our Mother: in the midst of this humanity, all of it your daughter, we who are the church of Jesus feel the need to ask your pardon and at the same time give you thanks as we complete these two thousand years of Christianity in history and in the hope of a new millennium more worthy of your heart and of humankind itself. We ask this for all those men and women who throughout these twenty Christian centuries have honoured the gospel with their lives and perhaps even their deaths, and in the name of all the poor of the earth, for whom the gospel of your Kingdom should be Good News indeed.

Virgilio Elizondo
Jon Sobrino

I · The Globalizing Evil of Our Actual World

Life and Death on Planet Earth

Leonardo Boff

The scenarios of the future of Earth are dramatic. Distinguished analysts admit that the present age in many ways resembles times of great rupture in the process of evolution, periods characterized by mass extinctions.[1] In effect, the human race is faced with an unparalleled situation. It has to decide whether to continue to live or choose its own self-destruction.

The risk comes not from any cosmic threat but from human activity itself. For the first time in the known process of hominization, human beings have provided themselves with the instruments of their own destruction. They have devised a principle of self-destruction, which has its counterpart in the principle of responsibility. From now on the existence of the biosphere is at the mercy of human decision-making. In order to continue to live, the human race has to wish to do so.

The indicators are alarming. They show that there is little time in which to make the changes needed. Optimistic estimates give a last date of the year 2030.[2] From then on, if urgent and effective measures are not taken, the sustainability of the Earth-system cannot be guaranteed.

Above all, we need wisdom: wisdom to understand the imperative changes; wisdom to define the right direction; wisdom to project the dream that will govern us; wisdom, finally, to prioritize the concerted actions that will transform this dream into reality.

I. The era of insanity

We are faced with three problematic knots, amongst others,[3] which need to be untied: the knot of the exhaustion of natural resources, the knot of

Earth's sustainability, and the knot of world-wide social injustice. Let us examine each in turn.

(a) The knot of the exhaustion of natural resources

Earth has been systematically plundered for centuries. Every day ten species of living creatures disappear. Since the time of the disappearance of the dinosaurs sixty-five million years ago, there has never been such a rapid diminution of living creatures. With them goes for ever a library of knowledge that nature had wisely put together.

Since 1972 the desertification of the world has advanced by an area equal to all the cultivated land in China and Nigeria together. Some 480 million tons of fertile soil have been lost, the equivalent of the agricultural land of France and India combined. The amount of land once cultivable has declined by sixty-five per cent. Extensive irrigation, together with widespread use of agricultural chemicals, has led to the salinization of waters unable to renew lost nutrients in time.

Half the world's forests standing in 1950 have been cut down. The last thirty years alone have seen the destruction of 600,000 square kilometres of the Brazilian Amazonian rainforest, an area the size of reunited Germany, or twice that of Congo.

The vast natural reservoirs of water formed over millions and millions of years have in the twentieth century been systematically drained and are on the point of drying up. At the beginning of the third millennium, drinking water will have become one of the scarcest natural resources. Wars are fought to guarantee access to sources of drinking water.

Petroleum and coal deposits, formed over a hundred million years in the bowels of the Earth, will have been exhausted by the middle of the next century. Both water and carbon were carefully buried by the Earth to stabilize its climate. They have now been dragged to the surface and returned to the atmosphere, producing imbalances we can still not measure adequately. By the year 2030 copper, bauxite, zinc, phosphate, and chromium will have been almost totally exhausted.

Behind this process of pillage lies a reductionist view of Earth. It is seen simply as a dead source of reserves to be exploited. It is not viewed as a super-system subtly articulated into systems and sub-systems in which rocks, waters, atmospheres, micro-organisms, other planets, animals, and human beings form an organic and dynamic whole with relationships of interdependence and synergy that guarantee the subsistence of each and every part. Earth is not respected in its otherness and autonomy, nor is it recognized as possessing any sacred character. Much less is it loved as a living super-organism, the Great Mother of the ancients, the Pacha Mama of the indigenous peoples of Latin America, or the Gaia of modern cosmologists. Human beings have always seen the Earth as something living; it is only in recent centuries that it has been seen as something inert, a disjointed whole made up of land (continents) and water (oceans, lakes and rivers).

(b) The knot of Earth's sustainability

How much aggression can Earth withstand without losing its inner equilibrium and self-destructing?

Acid rains are killing lakes and denuding forests. Chemical wastes are contaminating sources of drinking water and the oceans and poisoning soil. Pesticides are entering the food chain and affecting the health of living creatures and that of the generations to come. Nuclear waste is especially dangerous, as many substances will remain radioactive for the next hundred thousand years, and we are not within sight of any technology that can protect us against the damage it does.

The sixty thousand nuclear weapons built could, in the context of a world war, bring about the nuclear winter. The fine particles of smoke from the huge fires produced by them, together with the radioactive elements thrown into the atmosphere, would darken and cool the Earth to a greater degree than in the glacial periods of the Pleistocene epoch. The human race and the whole system of life would collapse – a consequence always ignored by militaristic powers. We now run the risk of terrorist groups having access to nuclear weapon technology and holding the human race and Earth to ransom.

The destruction of the ozone layer represents another great danger to the life of the planet. Lying in the stratosphere between thirty and fifty kilometres above Earth's surface, this acts as a shield protecting life against ultra-violet rays, which are lethal to all living organisms. The piercing of this ozone layer is produced by chlorofluorocarbons (CFCs). Chemically, these are an inert and harmless material used as liquids in refrigerators, air conditioning, deodorant sprays, insecticides, and so on. But once they reach the ozone layer in gaseous form, ultra-violet rays split their molecules, freeing chlorine, which destroys the ozone shield, thus exposing all living things to ultra-violet rays. These produce skin cancer, cataracts, weakening of the immune system, distortions of DNA, and damage to agriculture and the photosynthesis on which Earth's whole food chain depends.

Another major threat is global warming, the so-called 'greenhouse effect'. The burning of oil, coal and forests produces carbon dioxide, which, together with other gases such as methane, fluoride and nitrogen oxide, absorbs infra-red rays, forming a sort of hothouse, which warms the atmosphere. In the past century the earth's temperature has risen by between 0.3 and 0.6 degrees Celsius. The next hundred years are expected to show a rise of between 1.5 and 5.5 degrees. Such changes will produce massive disasters such as drought and the melting of the polar icecaps, with resultant flooding of the coastal areas in which sixty per cent of the world's population live, causing mass emigration or death. Many species of life will not adapt and will die out. The powerful greenhouse effect on Venus has been shown by the Russian space probe Venera: there the whole surface is burnt up by heat. Could Earth's greenhouse effect not produce similar consequences? Experts have been warning us of this possibility for some time.

What are Earth's powers of resistance in the face of so many assaults? Throughout the process of its formation, in which huge decimations of species have taken place (some eighty to ninety per cent in the Cambrian period some 570 million years ago), our planet has shown a great capacity for resistance and regeneration. Now, however, it is feared that the cumulative effect of so many assaults may reach a critical point at which the physical–chemical–biological equilibrium of Earth will snap. Huge catastrophes will affect the biosphere and cause the deaths of millions of human beings.[4]

(c) World-wide social injustice

Finally, just how much injustice and violence can the human spirit stand? It is unjust and pitiless that twenty per cent of humankind should enjoy eighty-three per cent of resources (in 1970 the figure was seventy per cent) while the poorest twenty per cent have only 1.4 per cent (2.3 per cent in 1960). It is unjust and cruel to keep a billion people in extreme poverty. It is unjust and perverse to let forty million people die simply from hunger every year. It is unjust, perverse, cruel and pitiless to tolerate fourteen million children dying every year before they are five days old.

This social cataclysm is neither natural nor innocent. It is the direct result of a form of economic, political and social organization that privileges some at the expense of the exploitation and destitution of the vast majorities. A type of development has evolved with no thought for its consequences for nature or for social relationships. This system is highly predatory and unequal, and is maintained through fear. To perpetuate itself, it makes permanent use of economic violence and of military aggression when needed. To do this, it spends $1,800,000 every minute on arms. It costs the countries of the southern hemisphere a Hiroshima and a Nagasaki in human lives every two days: 180,000 people sacrificed on the altar of the god Mammon (the global market), the equivalent of an atom bomb dropped every two days.[5]

The perverse effect of all this is undeniable: the great majority of the human race have no sustainability; they live a catastrophe day by day. Such violence constitutes an aggression against Earth, since human beings are Earth itself in its conscious and intelligent dimension.

So we ask once more: how much violence can Earth still tolerate without breaking as a system? Apart from having been suicidal, homicidal and ethnocidal in the past, we are now beginning to be ecocidal. Shall we end in the not too distant future by being geocidal?

II. We either change or destroy ourselves

At the present time we have reached a point where the characteristics of our paradigm of civilization are unable to take account of the problematic knots examined above. On the contrary, they make the situation worse and accelerate its destructive forces.

However, there are signs of hope. Since the beginning of the twentieth century, the modern paradigm has been – theoretically – beginning to be eroded by quantum physics, by the theory of relativity, by the new biology, by ecology, and by critical philosophy. A new paradigm is then taking shape: holistic, systemic, inclusive, pan-relational and spiritual in character. This understands the universe not as a thing or a juxtaposition of things and objects but rather as a subject in which everything has to do with everything else, at all points, in all circumstances, and in all directions, generating an immense cosmic solidarity.[6] Every being depends on others, sustains others, shares in the development of others, communing in one same origin, one same adventure, and one same common destiny.

The universe (from its original released energies and its most elementary particles to the human mind) forms a community of subjects, since all its components, the universe itself as an organic whole, are characterized by what forms a subject: interactivity, historicity, interiority and intentionality. This subject is inserted in an immense evolving, self-creating and self-organizing process made manifest in many forms, whether as matter and energy, information and complexity, or consciousness and interiority.

Instead of being seen as a universe made up of atoms, of discrete particles – a universe whose complexity has to be broken down into ever smaller and simpler components – this universe is now viewed as a relational whole, inter-retro-connected with everything and greater than the sum of its parts. The nature of matter, when analysed in greater depth, seems to be not something static and dead but rather a dance of energies and relationships going in all directions. Earth is no longer seen as a conglomerate of inert matter (the continents) and water (the oceans) but as a living super-organism, Gaia,[7] linking together all its elements: rocks, the atmosphere, living beings and consciousness in an organic, dynamic whole, radiating and full of purpose, part of an even greater whole that includes us: the universe in cosmogenesis, in expansion and shot through with consciousness.[8]

This vision furnishes us with the basis for a new hope, for a higher wisdom and for an alternative project of civilization. It allows us to move beyond the sensation of loss and fear induced by the present scenario to a feeling of belonging, promise and a better future.

Four axes give consistency to this new paradigm: the quest for ecological and economic *sustainability*, based on a new alliance of brother- and sisterhood with nature and among human beings; the welcoming of biological and cultural *diversity*, based on preservation of and respect for all differences and on the development of all cultures; the incentive to *participation* in social relationships and forms of government, inspired by democracy understood as a universal value to be experienced in all institutions (family, school, trade union, church, local and national politics) and with all the people; the cultivation of *spirituality* as an expression of human depth, of feeling oneself part of everything, capable of values of solidarity, compassion and dialogue with the originating Source of all beings.

This new paradigm is not yet dominant. That of modernity is still widespread – differentiating, mechanical, deterministic and dualistic, despite being refuted in theory and in practice. It lasts because it serves the purposes of the powers that dominate the world. They keep the mass of the people – and even highly educated people – in ignorance of the new vision of the world. The ruling order is still a global system whose major fruits are domination and destruction.

The global ecological crisis, however, provides us with a short-term stimulus we need for the necessary changes to confer immediacy and strength on the new paradigm. It is subversive of the current order. We need a new revolution: a civilizational revolution. This will be different in kind from all previous revolutions, starting with the Neolithic. It will have the new cosmology as its foundation and inspiration. But to bring it about we need to change our way of thinking, feeling, evaluating and acting. We need more wisdom than power, more veneration than knowledge, more humility than arrogance, more wish for synergy than self-affirmation, more desire to say *we* instead of *I*. With these attitudes, human beings will be able to save themselves and save their beautiful, radiant planet Earth.

I cling to the idea that we are in the birth pangs of a new level of hominization. Yes, we can destroy ourselves, and we have built a death-machine with which to do so. But this itself can be replaced and transformed: the giant rocket that carries nuclear warheads could be used to change the course of asteroids threatening the planet. This is the time to take a qualitative leap and inaugurate a new alliance with Earth. The chance has been created: it now depends on us whether its outcome is success or total failure. From now on we no longer have time to delay or to choose the wrong objective. There will be no new Noah's Ark to save some and leave the rest to perish. We all either sink or swim together.

I reject the notion that the 4.5 billion years of Earth's formation have been a preparation for its destruction. Its crises and suffering are heralds of a new dawn. No one can prevent this coming. A new civilizational revolution is being born and its first cries can already be heard. We are moving from an epoch of change to a change of epoch.

III. What dreams guide us?

A new civilization will arise when we find concrete answers to the following questions. What utopias will the future open to us? What new values will give meaning to our personal and social lives? What new practices will change our social relationships? What care shall we develop for nature, and what goodwill and compassion shall we apply to all the beings of creation? What new technologies shall we use so as not to deny poetry and grace? What brotherhood and sisterhood shall we establish among all peoples and cultures? What name shall we give to the Mystery that surrounds us, and with what symbols, feasts and dances shall we celebrate it? In a word: What are the dreams that give us hope?

Dreams are of major importance. Ideologies die, and philosophies grow old, but dreams remain. They are the soil in which we can continually plant new forms of social relationship or of dealings with nature. The Redskin Chief Seattle was right to write to Governor Stevens of Washington in 1856 when the latter forced through the sale of native land to the European colonizers. The Chief, rightly, could not understand why one should want to sell land, the breeze, the green of plants, the splendour of the landscape. In this context, he reflected that the Redskins might understand the purposes and civilization of the white men 'if they understood the dreams of the white man, if they knew what were the hopes he passed on to his sons and daughters in the long winter nights, and what visions of the future he had to offer for the following day'.

What is our dream? What hopes are we handing on to the young? What visions of the future are filling minds and the collective imagination through schools, the communications media, and our capacity for creating values?

The responses to such questions will generate a new pattern of civilizing activity. Coming down to the level of day-by-day activities, faced with the transformations that reach down to the roots of our present civilization, we need to ask: Who are the social subjects who will put forward a new historic dream and draw a new horizon of hope? And who are the collective subjects who will generate a new civilization? Broadly speaking, one can say that they are to be found in all cultures and in all quarters of the world. They come from all social strata and from all spiritual traditions. They are everywhere. But they are mainly those who feel dissatisfied with their present way of living, of working, of suffering, of rejoicing, and of dying, and they are mostly the excluded, the oppressed, the outcasts. These are the ones who, even though only a little step at a time, are teaching a new way of behaving and producing creative thoughts. They are also those who dare to organize themselves around certain desires, certain levels of consciousness, certain values, certain practices, and certain dreams and a certain veneration of the Mystery, and together they begin to create visions and convictions that irradiate a new vitality in everything they think, plan, do, and celebrate.

The new civilization is advancing along so many paths that from now on it will no longer be regional but collective and planetary and, it is to be hoped, more in solidarity, more ecological, more integrating, and more spiritual.

IV. The era of wisdom: the civilization of re-binding

What name shall we give to the new thing that is emerging? Let me try a reply: it will be a civilization more in tune with the basic law of the universe, which is pan-relationality, synergy and complementarity. It will be, in a word, a civilization of re-binding everything to everything and of everyone to everyone.[9] This is why it will be a civilization that gives a central place to *re-ligio*, to the body that proposes to re-bind everything together because it sees them umbilically re-bound to the Source of all being. This civilization will be re-ligious or it will be nothing. What type of religion – Western, Eastern, old, new – matters little, provided it is that radical experience that succeeds in re-binding all things and generating a sense of integration and wholeness. Then the civilization of the planetary age, of the society of Earth, can emerge, the first civilization of humankind as humanity.

We all need to feel ourselves wrapped in a single collective consciousness, in a single common responsibility, within one and the same Noah's Ark that is that blue-white spaceship Planet Earth. This new civilization is still only a goal, a smiling dream, but it is on its way. We only need to look at a powerful sign – the process of *globalization*.[10]

This is an irreversible process and undoubtedly represents a new phase in the history of Earth and the human race. We are on our way to the formation of a single world society, one that more and more needs a central direction in the questions that concern all human beings, such as food, health, housing, education, communication and the preservation of Earth.

It is true that we are still in the Iron Age of this process. We are in the phase of *competitive* globalization, which has not yet brought in *co-operative* globalization because it operates under the rule of capitalist *economics* and is therefore full of contradictions and conflicts, brought about rivalry, by the unchecked accumulation of wealth and quest for profit at any price, and so by a class struggle on a world-wide scale. This means of production, now globally established, makes everything merchandise, from human genes to information, from sex to mysticism. Merchandise, through marketing skills, has become a fetish to induce consumption and so bring profit.

We need a different economy, one built around production in sufficient quantity for all, human beings and the other living beings in creation. The present ruling economic model, of ever-increasing linear growth, does violence to Earth, is scarcely participative, and so unjust. But we shall only achieve a new political and economic order once a different scale of values predominates. As opposed to personal and collective egoism and individual and company profit, solidarity, participation and sharing have to prevail. Under the current model of competition and the triumph of the strongest, only one side wins. All the others lose. In the new – dreamed-of and possible – model, everyone wins and no one loses or is a victim of exclusion, since everything will be structured around synergy and co-operation. Then we shall indeed have co-operative globalization and societies in which there is room for all.

Whether we like it or not, the day is fast approaching when globalization is not only economic. It is also coming about under the sign of *ethics*, in the sense of universal compassion, in discovery of the human family and people of the most diverse origins as subjects having unconditional rights, rights that do not depend on the money we have in our purse, or the colour of our skin, or the religion we profess, or what football team we support. We shall all be under the same rainbow of solidarity, of respect for a valuation of differences and moved by feelings of universal love for all our brothers and sisters.

We also need to construct power relationships in the *political* sphere, no longer on the basis of domination/exploitation of people and nature but in the form of biophilic mutuality (reciprocity among living beings) and of collaboration among all peoples, the basis for collective living in justice, peace and brotherly/sisterly alliance with nature. This should be organized around a common goal: to guarantee the future of the Earth-system and the conditions in which human beings can continue to live and to develop, as they have been doing for some ten million years.

Finally, there will be a globalization of experience of the *Spirit* through cultivation of the spiritual energies that pervade the universe, work in the depths of human minds and cultures, and reinforce synergy, solidarity and love of life, working from the most disadvantaged and veneration of the ineffable Mystery that generates everything, permeates everything, and keeps everything in being.

We are facing an experiment unprecedented in the history of the human race. If the future is to become present, it cannot be a continuation of the past. This would lead us to the fate of the dinosaurs, which suddenly died out.

This is the great lesson we have to learn: we either change or we perish. We either follow the road to Emmaus, sharing with and giving hospitality to all the inhabitants of spaceship Earth, or we follow that to exile in Babylon, a road of tribulation and desolation. This time there will be no Noah's Ark to save some and let others perish. We have no right to delude ourselves about the gravity of our situation.

Meanwhile a hope that cannot be turned aside persists. Since vertebrates emerged 157 million years ago, followed by *homo sapiens* and *demens*, Earth has known fifteen great decimations in which its biotic capital was almost extinguished. But life has always triumphed, has always been able to re-make itself. As in a sort of vendetta against evolution itself, biodiversity has grown. This logical evolutionary targeting still holds good in the present situation. So we can have a well-grounded hope that life will triumph over death as it always has done. The balance between life and death is dynamic and always open to allowing the sym-bolic to overcome the dia-bolic and life to prevail over death.

Translated by Paul Burns

Notes

1. C. de Duve, *Vital Dust*, New York 1995: the whole of ch. 30, 'The Future of Life'.
2. Cf. R. Radford Reuther, *Gaia and God: An Eco-Feminist Theology of Earth's Healing*, San Francisco and London 1992, 86.
3. There are many sources of data on the ecological–social crisis: see, e.g., the 'Worldwatch Papers' and 'State of the World' published since 1984 by the Worldwatch Institute, Washington; L. Boff, *Ecology and Liberation*, Maryknoll, NY 1995; E. Drewermann, *Der tödliche Fortschritt*, Regensburg 1997, ch. 1, 'Facts that are Symptoms'; M. D. Hathaway, *Transformative Education. Awakening Humanity to the Challenge of the Global Crisis*, Scarborough (Ontario) 1993; and the United Nations Development Reports published annually by the UN and containing statistics on the social situation of the world.
4. P. Ward, *The End of Evolution*, New York 1995.
5. Cf. R. Garaudy, *Le débat du siècle*, Paris 1996, 7.
6. For all this see the classic T. Berry and B. Swimme, *The Universe Story. From the Primordial Faring-forth to the Ecozoic Age: A Celebration of the Unfolding of the Cosmos*, San Francisco 1992; T. Berry, *The Dream of the Earth*, San Francisco 1988; D. Zohar and I. Marshall, *The Quantum Society: Mind, Physics and a New Social Vision*, New York 1994; S. Hawking, *A Brief History of Time: From the Big Bang to the Black Holes*, London and New York 1988.
7. Cf. J. Lovelock, *Gaia: A New Look at Natural History*, Oxford 1997; id., *The Ages of Gaia: A Biography of Our Living Earth*, New York 1988; E. Sahtouris, *Earth Dance: Living Systems in Evolution*, New York 1996.
8. See the thesis of the well-known quantum physicist and his team: E. Goswami, R. E. Reed and M. Goswami, *The Self-aware Universe: How Consciousness Creates the Material World*, New York 1993.
9. L. Boff, *Cry of the Earth, Cry of the Poor*, Maryknoll, NY 1997, the whole of ch. 6.
10. E. Morin, *Terre-Patrie*, Paris 1993; L. Boff, *Ethische Herausforderungen der Globalisierung*, Basel University 1998.

Some Specific Cases

1. The Situation of Africa

Elizabeth Amoah

The general impression one gets from the current situations in Africa is that many African nations seem to be pushed and strangled by a series of crises. These include economic, political, social and religious causes. Consequently, a high rate of unemployment in the towns, the catastrophe of AIDS/HIV, poverty and the most murderous civil wars are some of the current realities in Africa. Political and social analysts have strongly argued that the imposition of the IMF/World Bank, with the antecedent Structural Adjustment Programmes and other factors such as low commodity prices, a ruthless free market and the debt burden, are also dissipating Africa's rich resources and further deepening the gloomy situation.

This scenario has led to the ever-rising cost of living, the falling prices of raw materials, the over-exploitation of natural resources, an increase of the gap between the rich and the poor and a curb in social services (education, health) in many African societies. The mortality rate and morbidity, especially of children and women, are also increasing. Family units, especially in the urban areas, are breaking down at a fast rate. Abuse and violence (cultural, social, economic, gender and spiritual), especially to women, are common realities in many African societies. It seems as if enormous crises upon crises have become endemic and widespread in Africa and this has attracted the attention of the media, social scientists, historians and theologians. Professor Julius Ihonvbere, for example, says that: 'the list of Africa's woes can go on endless and many scholars have a career of frequently cataloguing these woes.'[1] Ihonvbere may sound cynical, but the truth still remains that many African nations are today confronted with endless crisis. In Africa, many lives are needlessly destroyed and wasted through disease, hunger, poverty and wars, which can only be described as carnage.

Although the present situations in many African societies south of the Sahara seem very gloomy and hopeless, I believe that Africa is a rich continent, especially in terms of human and natural resources, when it gives more to the world than it receives. In a recent paper, Ann Pettifor[2] argued that every year, the poorest countries in Africa pay over 12 billion dollars as debt service to the donor countries in the West. Again, she intimated that until recently Mozambique, a country which has been declared the poorest in the world, was paying 130 million dollars a year on loans which were probably used to pay for deadly military equipment for the prolonged war. Obviously the interest rate on Africa's debt is extremely high and the conditions attached to the loans are unmanageable.

We are told, for instance, that on each dollar received as aid, the indebted African nations pay an average of eleven dollars as debt service. Such a continent, which sends more money out than it receives, cannot be said to be a poor continent. Rather, both external and internal unjust systems coupled with other factors make Africa a poor continent.

In the attempt to service the huge and endless debt, the debt-ridden nations in Africa have had to devise harsh economic measures, which have devastating effects on human lives. For example, it has been estimated that while an average person in Africa may have to pay about twenty-two dollars to service national debt, the nations spend an average of eleven dollars on health facilities for each person. In my own country, Ghana, the picture is indeed very gloomy, for while the government spends only four dollars on health facility on each person, it pays twenty-seven dollars per person in debt service. Many African countries, including Ghana, have had to withdraw subsidies on social services.

Two-thirds of the estimated number of people infected with AIDS/HIV are said to be in African countries south of the Sahara which cannot even spend more than twenty dollars a year on health care for one person! AIDS/HIV, as we know, is not the only menacing disease in Africa. Malaria is another deadly disease, which takes the lives of many persons each day. The consequence of such a gloomy situation is that thousands of people who constitute a large portion of the labour force die daily, and countless numbers of children are made orphans while families and nations helplessly look on. As an illustration of this gloomy picture, it has been estimated that by the year 2010, the number of adults with AIDS in Uganda will rise to 1.7 million (World Bank 1991).

The debt crisis has a telling effect on the agriculture sector as well. In their effort to service the huge debt, many African nations concentrate more on export items such as cocoa, coffee and flowers for the much-needed hard currency than on basic food items such as maize, plantain and yam. The fact is that Ghanaians cannot eat the large quantities of cocoa the farmers have been encouraged to plant year after year. Similarly, Kenyans, and for that matter everyone else, cannot eat the flowers that they are encouraged to grow for export. And yet in order to continue to be the 'success story' of the international financial institutions, Ghana continues to grow cocoa even thought its price is steadily falling on the world market.

More importantly, however, Ghanaians or Kenyans do not have any say in the price of cocoa or the flowers they export abroad. It is the buyers, mostly from the Western countries, who decide on the price of the export items. The global market is certainly not free for many African nations. For while non-African countries can sell their goods, food, second-hand clothing and other items without restriction, say, to Ghana, Ghana cannot freely expert her bananas outside Africa.

The government of Ghana is again revamping the mining sector for hard currency to pay her debts. As such, there is an increase in private and small-scale mining industries, particularly in the rural areas where most of the agricultural activities take place. Naturally, many of the farmlands including those with food crops have been taken over by these private companies with very little compensation to the farmers. In Ghana, there is a prolonged problem between the multi-national mining company, the Ashanti GoldFields Company, and some cocoa farmers in Ashanti over the issue of the payment of compensation.[3] In all this, the fact remains that at the end of the day; the farmers and their families will remain poorer while the mining companies become richer.

Besides, through the uncontrolled small-scale mining activities, known in Ghana as *garamsey* (get it and sell it), rivers are being polluted with the deadly chemical mercury, used by young and unskilled miners to separate the gold particles from the soil. In my village, Mpoho, the miners indiscriminately fell trees and this means that the rich arable lands are eventually rendered infertile and useless for farming. One can only imagine the long term and the devastating effect on the ecology and the food situation in my village and in the country as a whole.

The point I am trying to make is that the economic policies of many debt-ridden African nations, coupled with other factors, have naturally contributed to the perennial food crisis on the African continent. The cost of the scarce food is extremely high and the children of those who cannot afford to buy the basic essential food die every day of malnourishment.

This gloomy situation is even made worse in African nations where genocidal wars are rampant. Political instability due to oppressive and corrupt governments, boundary and land disputes, ethnic and religious conflicts have resulted in wars and encouraged militarism which, in my view, is one of the realities in Africa. For it undoubtedly intensifies conflict and genocidal wars in which innocent and helpless people are displaced and traumatized. There are indeed countless women and children who have been raped and tortured, displaced and traumatized through war. Countless refugees in deplorable conditions are scattered all over Africa. For example, it is currently estimated that there are 40,000 Burundi, 160,000 Angolans, 111,000 Sudanese and 18,500 Ugandans, etc. who are refugees in the Democratic Republic of Congo alone.[4] In such situations, the perpetrators of conflict in the war zones invariably use the scarce hard currencies to buy deadly and very expensive weapons to keep themselves in power.

In Liberia and Sierra Leone it has been observed that instead of being in schools, a number of children have become warlords and are burdened with deadly and sophisticated weapons that literally weigh them down. Thus, in a recent *Scottish Daily Mail*, David William reporting on the recent situation in Sierra Leone writes:

> An estimated 44,000 have died and 45% of the country's four million people are displaced. A generation of child soldiers whose crimes include cannibalism, have grown up with blood on their hands.
>
> In one recent incident, women and children were rounded up and locked in a house which was then set ablaze. In another, men who refused to rape members of their own family had their ears and arms hacked off.[5]

A further consequence of such genocidal wars is that millions of people have needlessly died or have been reduced to nothing but moving skeletons. I have in mind cases of millions of children and women in war situations in places such as Sudan, Somalia, Rwanda, Liberia and Sierra Leone.

While people are needlessly dying of hunger and menacing diseases, some African governments spend the scarce hard currency to acquire deadly weapons. In a recent news item in the *Daily Mail*, it was reported that the governments of Uganda and Zimbabwe have respectively spent about 35 and 54 million dollars on military hardware as a result of the devastating conflict in the Democratic Republic of Congo.[6] Again, in the *Scottish Daily Mail*, 7 December 1997, Brian James intimated that recently the war-torn Sierra Leone was paying the Executive Outcomes, a mercenary company, $1.7 million dollars a month[7] in the name of 'peace keeping', while lives and property were being destroyed. This, for me, is indeed evil; it challenges us urgently to search for visions which hopefully will sensitize people to deal fairly and justly with each other.

In search of such visions, I shall reflect on some of the resilient features of the Akan cultural heritage to which I belong. From the traditional Akan cultural heritage with its strong emphasis on the sense of community, the situations outlined above would seem to be evil because the victims are completely denied their identities as children of God. The Akan would describe such perpetuators of the evils in society as *wonnye nimpa*; that is, they are not human beings, for they do not fear God, *wonnsoro Nyame*. In other words, in the view of the Akan, to be truly human is to be accountable to God and the community at large and to treat persons with dignity and respect. That is to say that the concern for the well-being of humanity supercedes ruthless search for material gains. Again, the idea is that persons are so closely inter-connected and inter-related with each other that what one does, seems to affect all. Thus, the Akan say,

ani nya a na ehwene anya,

which means, what affects the eye, affects the nose. Another saying is,

Wo nyonko wuda ne wo da.[8]

This means, 'The day your neighbour dies is the day you die.'

The point is that the whole community is affected by what happens to one member. Thus, it is a community of people that holds the strong view that one's business is the business of all the members. Hence, a person who tends to please himself or herself regardless of the effect of the individual's actions on the entire community is described as not fearing God, *onnsuro Nyame*,[9] that is, he or she does not fear God. Of course, this must be seen in the Akan cultural context, which sees God as the centre and the source of the well-being of all persons and the entire community. In the traditional Adan world-view, living in harmony with God, nature and fellow members of the community implies seeing one's actions as affecting not only oneself alone but also all members of the community. It implies supporting and building each other up. In this sense, the Akan see the material wealth of individuals who become filthily rich with the sweat of others as being unclean, *sika fi*, which means unclean money. No one, no matter how poor that person is, will be interested in such 'filthy wealth'.

From this perspective, then, the search is an anthropological, ethical and a theological task, which puts to test our maturity as human beings.

It is a search for re-defining our humanity and our relationship with God and with each other. Otherwise, our noble ventures, our well-thought-out strategic plans and policies may, invariably, end in the same way as the proverbial project of the tower of Babel ended. From Genesis the builders of the tower of Babel were so obsessed with making names for themselves that they might have forgotten God, the source of being. The tower to heaven naturally collapsed and there was a complete breakdown of communication.

Being in constant tune with the source of all life will hopefully enable persons to realize, as did the traditional Akan, that as human beings with a common Source of being, 'the day one's neighbour dies, is the day one dies'. For me, this realization is in line with the concept of Jubilee, a time to pause, to reflect on what God demands of God's people and to move on to a renewed future. The renewed future cannot be totally actualized if the rich financial institutions just cancel debts. On the international level, the high interest rate and the unmanageable conditions attached to loans need to be reduced and removed respectively. There should be a strong body to control the financial institutions whose unrestricted activities trickle down to people at the grass-roots level, just as there are bodies to check undemocratic and oppressive governments.

Most importantly, African nations and governments should be accountable and learn to govern themselves well. It is time for those in leadership positions in Africa to realize that politics is neither a form of 'gold rush' nor an avenue for self-fulfilment. Political leaders should have the humility to see their work as service to the electorate and not as an opportunity to settle scores with political opponents. The sensitivity for human dignity can be possible if persons realize that each and every one is accountable to God and that the day a neighbour dies is the day one dies.

Notes

1. J. O. Ihonvbere, 'Pan-Africanism: Agenda for African Unity in the 1990's?', *Issues and Trends in Contemporary African Politics: Stability, Development and Democratization*, ed. George Akeya Agbango, New York 1997, 350.
2. A. Pettifor, 'Debt as Bondage: Africa's Relations with International Creditors', University of Edinburgh, 4 November 1998.
3. Joy Online, *Business and Financial Report*, 9 November 1998.
4. UNHCR's Special Programme in the Greater Lakes Region, 1998.
5. *Daily Mail*, 16 May 1998.
6. *Daily Mail*, 24 November 1998.
7. 'Night and Day', *The Mail on Sunday Review*, 7 December 1997, 27.
8. E. Amoah, *The Akan Traditional Concept of the Household*, a paper presented at

a workshop organized by The Circle of African Women Theologians in Nairobi, 1996.

9. *Nyame* is the Akan word for the creator god who is believed to be the source of all life.

2. The Mayas of Chiapas

Carlos Mendoza-Álvarez

I. The frontier of death

The Mayas invented the zero, and their genius has lived on in world culture since then. Zero is the abstract concept of the universal point of reference, and on it they based their cities and their astronomical calculations. The great cities of Chichen-Itzá, Uxmal and Mayapán are symbols of the high degree of social, political and religious organization they achieved on the basis of an affluent economic empire not exempt from slavery and oppression.

When Fray Bartolomé de Las Casas arrived in Maya territory in 1545 – the year of the opening of the Council of Trent – as first bishop of Chiapas, this august civilization had disappeared, probably extinguished by internal political struggles in the depths of the jungle. Using the techniques of Renaissance model-city foundations, several friars devoted themselves to reorganizing social life around new towns in which the good Central American India would appear as an alternative to the decadent world of Europe.

(a) Ethnocide

The Mayan Indian peoples, made up of more than ten distinct clans but unified by a common ancestral culture, then went through five centuries of resistance and exploitation as the 'dimly burning wick' (Isa. 42.3).

It was above all in the nineteenth century, in now independent Mexico, that the Mayan peoples suffered an atrocious campaign of exploitation carried out by English and German loggers who hacked down the hardwood forests to sell the mahogany and other valuable woods that grew along the river Lacantún in the markets of London.[1]

(b) Social intolerance

The Mexican revolution of 1910 came late and cold to the heights of Chiapas and to its rain forests bordering on Guatemala. Its campaigns for 'land and freedom', carried out by peasants from central Mexico led by Zapata and by ranchers from the north of the country led by Villa, achieved some results in areas of mixed populations, but none in the more remote Indian lands belonging to the fifty-six indigenous ethnic groups who still live in Mexico today.

The social intolerance from which the Maya Indians suffered has already been magisterially recounted by Rosario Castellanos, the great twentieth-century novelist of the castes of Chiapas. To be Indian was synonymous with being sub-human, according to the unfortunate translation of *physei doulos*, the 'slaves by nature' of Aristotle's *Politics*, made by Ginés de Sepúlveda in his polemic against Las Casas in 1548, the same that produced the theoretical justification for the subjection of the American Indians through the institution of the *encomienda*.[2]

(c) Cultural exclusion

The Mexican revolution became 'institutionalized' in a system of government that has lasted since the 1920s. With its presumed basis of popular support, the ideology of the modern Mexican state exalted the Indians in its cast of idyllic images but excluded them from land, production and modernization through a series of forced marches that has been going on since the 1940s. The National Indigenist Institute (INI) was founded during this period with the aim of preserving Indian cultures, but in effect subjecting them to the *mestizo* power in use of language, to the juridical practices of Romano–Germanic law, and to Western systems of industrial production. Bilingual education, although proposed as a criterion for action by the INI, together with defence of the human rights of indigenous peoples of Mexico through procurement of a special system of justice, proved to be declarations of good intent rather than effective instruments for promoting Indian cultures.

In 1974, as a result of the first indigenous congress, convened by the bishop of San Cristóbal de Las Casas, Mgr Samuel Ruiz García, the Mayan communities of Chiapas began to arise from their centuries-old lethargy and to wake up to the undeniable value of their dignity on the national and international scene. During the following decades the work of community organization – through co-operatives for production, commerce and purchasing, linked to literacy and evangelization campaigns, carried out in various social sectors – fused into a social movement with a clear purpose of promoting the rights of the Indian peoples.

II. Signs of life

(a) Enough is enough!

On 1 January 1994 the North American Free Trade Area (NAFTA) came into being, making a reality of the ruling elite's dream cherished through years of apparent macro-economic prosperity. On the morning of that very day the uprising by the Zapatista Army of National Liberation (EZLN) began, using the slogan *¡Ya basta! ¡Para todos, todo! ¡Nada para nosotros!* ('Enough is enough! Everything for everyone! Nothing for ourselves!').[3] Within a few months the EZLN had gathered around itself a social movement of global implication, which saw the indigenous-*mestizo* uprising as a post-modern sign of critique of the economic system of globalization and of the strident free-marketeering that has left the poorest of the poor – the Indian peoples – out in the cold.

The ideology of this movement has found an echo in the numerous proposals of non-governmental organizations campaigning for human rights and a new international order in which the third generation of human rights (those of peoples) would be recognized and applied to indigenous autonomies within those states that have seriously damaged these peoples under the Western model of the nation state.

(b) Indian theology

In the religious sphere, the appearance of the Indian peoples has brought new developments. The Christian communities are seeking to generate processes of inculturating the faith in an Indian *logos*, with celebrations linked to the land and its life-cycles, community ministries, complementarity of men and women, a social and prophetic dimension to faith, and ecumenical encounter with both ancestral and historical religions.[4]

The source of Indian Christian theology is the faith of their fathers who received the gospel of Jesus Christ in these lands and put it into practice in their community life, as well as in their prayers and pilgrimages, their petitions and their customs of community government, with leaders performing unpaid tasks in turns.

Mayan religious experience is marked by the confluence of a mysticism of rites of sacred communion (sacraments, saints, sacred places) with a strong social charge of commitment to attending to the needs of the weakest, explicitly prophetic in inspiration. The theology of Christ-*ceiba* – tree of life in his wood of the cross planted in the ground to make it fruitful and joyful – is a specific example of development of a language that properly belongs to the Nazarene while being based on a Mayan symbolic-anthropological re-reading. The ministry of *tuhuneles*, or community servants, in the *tseltal* Mayan church,[5] which has now become an official rank within the diaconate, performs leadership functions among the *tseltal* communities, with a pastoral and counselling role like that of the ancients, its ministers equally proven in their capacity for work for the communities entrusted to them.

(c) The martyrs of Acteal

On 22 December 1998 forty-five Maya Indians – women and children with their catechists – were shot in the back as they were praying for peace at a shrine in the municipal district of Polhó in Chiapas.[6] Members of a cooperative called *Las Abejas*, 'The Bees', they were victims of the ravages of the underground war waged by the federal army and paramilitary groups against the social bases of the EZLN since 1994. They had chosen non-violent means and had not allowed themselves to be intimidated by the spiralling violence in those parts. Their deaths marked a watershed in the history of the conflict in Chiapas and beyond, since it not only unmasked the iniquity of a system that perverts the values of the Kingdom of God in order to serve the interests of those in power but also, to an exceptional degree, revealed the truth of those who seek to build an alternative world and so, in their own flesh, put a stop to the violence of this world.

The theological significance of the martyrs of Acteal has yet to be taken on board by the church in Mexico. Ultimately, it leads to the intelligence of the victim,[7] as revealed in Jesus of Nazareth and all the just in history, showing us how it is possible to change this corrupt world, not with the force of violence but through the dignity of those who love and hope for a fullness from beyond: history under the mark of Cain that calls us forward together to continue opening it to the history of Abel and the just.

III. Questions to the Western rationale

(a) For an ethic of life

The word of the Maya peoples at this turn of millennium is a proposal of hope in the era of hyper-valuation of the global village and electronic market place. The Mayas' dramatic micro-history of discrimination and dignity is a paradoxical lesson for all the peoples of the world.

This is not a question of clinging to a victim mentality, with a feverish thirst for vengeance against executioners of any sort. While there is a clear component of clamour for justice, there is none of destructive resentment. In successive national congresses of the Indian peoples of Mexico, in national and international gatherings, the Mayas have put forward a new social pact in which there is room for all diversities of race, religion and gender.

The criteria for postulating an ethic of life from out of the experience of oppression-liberation have been acutely expressly by Enrique Dussel in his most recent work.[8] It is, in effect, a matter of setting out, at this time of globalization and exclusion, the formal principles of an ethic whose contents will materially include defence of life, especially of the life of the other who is threatened, dispossessed and disfigured by the mechanisms of economic exploitation, social discrimination and cultural exclusion. Without this material referent – the life of the other in constant growth – there can be no possible consensus or verification or communication, as the Frankfurt school candidly indicated and all our end-of-century communication skills confirm.

(b) Human diversity

The *oikumene* to which the Indian Mayan peoples are calling us is that of a plural and tolerant society in which there is room for all possible human worlds: that is, for all the faces that utter a true word.

From the depths of denial of the face of the Indian other, his prophetic voice, as in the times of Israel's captivity, is a cry for a new creation that will benignly welcome the gift of the God who is drawing near. Messianic times in the history of the poor are, then, the call of this ancestral voice. This is not a matter of now legitimizing, with an ingenuous a-critical approach, any social system in the name of God or of the faith as the only viable and legitimate means of ordering the human and ecological community. It is rather a question of achieving hope once more on the basis of the call of the innocent to imagine new worlds where there will be no more covering-up of the other but rather discovery-of and meeting-with others (individuals, peoples, nations) as a sign of the living and consoling presence of Jesus, the Messiah.

(c) Images of God

Finally, the Christian faith as inculturated in the Maya world is as expression of eco-human communion: bound to the earth without sacralizing it, while raising one's hands to the God of life who has compassion on his suffering yet hope-bearing people.

The prophetic outreach of this people – poor, believing, and full of dignity – has been nourished by the first fathers in faith in these lands, such as the intrepid sixteenth-century evangelizer Pedro Lorenzo de la Nada. Continuing the bold spirit of this preacher, when no one believed in his word or in his conviction that he had to go deeper into the jungle to meet the Indian other, today the Mayan peoples are still saying that in there, in the heart of the forest – a metaphor redolent of mystery – there is an Otherness who waits for us to make us all brothers and sisters. But in order to reach that place we have to leave behind all ties to unjust and inhuman slavery. Friar Pedro Lorenzo set out, even against the order of his prior, and was lost in the *nada*, the nothingness . . . where he met the Other.

Translated by Paul Burns

Notes

1. J. de Vos, *El oro verde*, Mexico City 1990.
2. E. O'Gorman, 'La idea antropológica del padre Las Casas', *Historia mexicana*, 16/3, Mexico City 1967, 315–16.
3. EZLN, *Primera declaración de la selva lacandona*, Mexico City 1994, 15ff.
4. See especially the publications of the National Centre for Aid to Indigenous Missions (CENAMI), *Teología india mayense*, Mexico City 1993; E. Maurer, 'El cristianismo tseltal', in M. Marzal (ed.), *El rostro indio de Dios*, Mexico City 1994, 89–132.
5. P. Iríbarren, *Vino nuevo en odres nuevos*, Mexico City 1997, 21–34.
6. 'Fray Bartolomé de Las Casas' Centre for Human Rights, *Acteal: entre el duelo y la lucha*, Mexico City 1998.
7. A concept refined by J. Alison, inspired by R. Girard, to understand the mechanisms for overcoming mimetic violence, which Jesus of Nazareth pioneered in history as the chief sign of the new life offered by God to all. See J. Alison, *The Joy of Being Wrong, Original Sin through Easter Eyes*, New York 1997, 139–61.
8. E. Dussel, *La ética de la liberación en la edad de la globalizatión y de la exclusión*, Madrid/Mexico City 1998.

3. 'Death Row' USA

John Mannion

Having a parishioner on death row has caused me to ask two questions: 1. Why does the US retain the death penalty, while other countries are abolishing it? 2. Is the death penalty immoral in itself, and if so, why are so many Catholics in favour of it?

In the US, there are links from slavery to the present. The Civil War was fought by the Southern States to retain slavery which was abolished in 1865, but it took another amendment (1868) to guarantee freed slaves citizenship, yet another (1871) to guarantee them the right to vote, and Civil Rights were only achieved under the leadership of Martin Luther King in the 1960s. Between the Civil War and the Civil Rights movement, approximately 5,000 black men were lynched. Between 1930 and 1972, 1,712 whites and 2,035 blacks were executed for murder or rape at a time when blacks constituted 9–11% of the population. In 1972 the US Supreme Court abolished the death penalty, but reinstated it in 1976, under pressure from the Southern States. From 1977 to 1995 Texas has led all other states in executions (104), followed by Florida (36), Virginia (29), Louisiana (22), Georgia (20) and Missouri (17), all of them Southern States. In 1997 alone, Texas executed 37 people, a number which equals the combined total for all other Death Penalty States.[1]

The death penalty represents the tip of the iceberg of a badly flawed justice system in a racist culture. Today, the US locks up more of its citizens than most nations on earth. Since 1980, America's prison population has more than tripled from 500,000 to 1.7 million, due largely to drug and alcohol abuse and addiction, with blacks making up more than 42% of the prison population.[2]

The race factor. In 1995, of 3,054 prisoners on death row, 43% were black or minority. In 1997, the American Bar Association called for a moratorium on the use of the death penalty, calling it 'a haphazard maze of unfair practices'.[3] An international Commission of Jurists (1996) concluded that: (*a*) racial prejudice influences the imposition of the death penalty and (*b*) elected judges lack the independence necessary to protect constitutional and human rights in capital cases. The US General

Accounting Office (1990) concluded that 'the race of the *victim* was found to influence the likelihood of being charged with capital murder . . . a finding remarkably consistent across data sets, states, data collection methods, and analytic techniques'.

Poverty. While the rich buy their way out of the system, the poor depend on court-appointed lawyers with little experience in capital cases. In at least three cases in Texas, lawyers have slept during capital trials, but the courts ruled that this did not violate the constitutional right to counsel because 'the Constitution doesn't say the lawyer has to be awake', a decision upheld by the US Supreme Court. Thirty-five years ago, twenty-seven Attorneys General supported a petition before the Supreme Court in support of the poor having the right to a lawyer. Last year, the National Association of Attorneys General successfully campaigned to eliminate such funding. It is more important to get on with executions than it is to ensure that justice be done.[4]

Prosecutorial discretion. In the US a prosecutor is *never required* to seek the death penalty in *any case* whatsoever. Harris County, which includes Houston, has a higher number of death penalty convictions than any other state except for Texas itself, with 134 inmates on death row due to its prosecutor. Individual prosecutors have been identified who have used the majority of their jury challenges against black jurors, thus ensuring that blacks are tried and condemned by white prosecutors and juries.

Arbitrariness. Out of 20,000 homicides annually in the US, on average the death penalty is imposed on 250 or 1 in 80 cases.

Innocence. A 1987 study published by the Stanford Law Review found at least 350 persons were mistakenly convicted of potential capital crimes between 1900 and 1985. Of these innocent people 130 were sentenced to death and 23 were executed. Since 1973, 75 people sentenced to death have been released due to proof of innocence. They had been on average 7 years on death row. The Supreme Court in 1972 stopped executions, citing among factors the risk of executing the innocent, but in Herrera v. Collins (1993) the same court ruled that innocence is irrelevant if it had not been determined in the original trial.

Mental retardation. Since 1976, at least 27 mentally retarded defendants have been executed. The Supreme Court in Penry v. Lynaugh (1989) ruled that the Eighth Amendment does not prohibit execution of the mentally retarded. Coincidentally 27 states, including Texas, allow such killings, and approximately 12–20% of death row prisoners are in this category.

Mental illness. The Supreme Court in Ford v. Wainwright (1986) ruled that the Eighth Amendment prohibits execution of the insane, but if they can be made sane by medical treatment, it is OK to kill them. The term 'insane' has been so narrowly defined that all 38 states which have the death penalty routinely execute people with serious mental illnesses.

Children. The US is one of only five countries (Saudi Arabia, Iran, Iraq and Yemen are the others) that since 1990 have executed prisoners who were under eighteen at the time of the crime. It leads the world in the execution of children.[5] The Supreme Court in Thompson v. Oklahoma (1988) ruled that sixteen-year-olds can be executed. There is a thirteen-year-old who has been sentenced to life without parole in the US for a capital offence. In Texas, Johnny Frank Garrett was seventeen when he was convicted and sentenced to death. On death row, he was diagnosed as paranoid schizophrenic, had auditory and visual hallucinations and had been repeatedly sexually abused as a child. He was executed in Huntsville, Texas, in 1992.

Lack of an independent judiciary. The 'tough on crime' slogan is used to good effect by politicians. Governors in California and Tennessee have advocated voting out of office judges deemed to be 'soft on crime', and both the current and past occupants of the White House have used the death penalty to good effect during the election process.

Ambivalence in Catholicism. As a pastor loyal to my church, I struggle with apparent inconsistencies in my church's position on the issue. Our history is disturbing. Before Constantine, there is abundant evidence of pacifism,[6] but the election of Damasus I (366) marked a profound about turn on the issue of killing. He hired a mob which killed 137 followers of his rival Ursinus.[7] In 385/386 Christians killed Christians in the name of doctrinal orthodoxy (the execution of Priscillian of Avila) and Leo I (440–461) endorsed it. When the Crusaders captured Jerusalem, they burned the synagogue with the Jews trapped inside.

Pope Innocent III's (1198–1218) crusade against the Albigensians, headed by the Cistercian General Arnald Almaric, slaughtered between 7,000 and 20,000 men, women and children in the town of Beziers. Simon de Montfort continued the war and kept the Pope fully informed of all developments. In one letter to de Montfort, the Pope praised and thanked God 'for that which He has mercifully wrought through you and through these others whom zeal for the orthodox faith has kindled to this work against His most pestilential enemies'.[8] From action to justification is but a step and, in a profession of faith imposed on supposed heretics, we find the first official justification of killing: 'the secular power can, without moral sin, exercise judgment of blood, provided that it punishes with justice, not out of hatred, with prudence, not precipitation' (1210).[9]

Gregory IX wrote (1227): 'It is the duty of every Catholic to persecute heretics', and established the Roman Inquisition (1232) for that purpose.

Torture was sanctioned by Innocent IV (1252) in the Bull *Ad extirpenda*. Heretics could be burned at the stake; those who repented were to be imprisoned for life. St Thomas Aquinas, writing against this background, became one of the standard justifications for the death penalty. In the *Summa Theologica* (2a, 2ae, 64.2) he writes: 'To kill a man who retains his natural dignity is intrinsically evil, although it may be justifiable to kill a sinner just as it is to kill a beast, for, as Aristotle points out, an evil man is worse than a beast and more harmful' (2a, 2ae 64.4). Clerics are entrusted with the ministry of the New Law which lays down no capital or corporal punishment.

To understand this teaching, so totally out of character for a man of such profound spirituality, it must be remembered that he was eight when the Roman Inquisition was established, and twenty-seven when torture was sanctioned, so it would have been absolutely impossible for him as a teacher and writer to call into question the morality of the death penalty. To quote him in defence of its use is to miss the extent to which his historical situation limited his freedom.

Interestingly Protestants found nothing objectionable in the death penalty either. The Spanish Inquisition killed about 3,000 heretics, but under English law about 20,000 witches were killed. Total killing of witches, Catholic and Protestant, has been estimated at between 200,000 and 500,000. The death penalty was only removed from the Vatican statutes in 1969.

An outcry greeted the 1992 Catechism's claim as 'the right and duty of legitimate public authority . . . (to use) the death penalty'.[10] Cardinal Ratzinger stated (1997) that in a revision it would be excluded 'in every case without exception', but this did not happen. The new edition cites the traditional teaching and says that 'cases in which the execution of the offender is absolutely necessary are rare, if not practically non-existent'. The implication is that killing by the state is not wrong in itself. Professor Rocchio[11] has argued that the Catechism's position is 'sophisticated, subtle and global'. It certainly is. On the one hand it agrees with the European Court of Human Rights that 'the death penalty is no longer consistent with regional standards of justice', while on the other hand implying that the church has not changed its position on the intrinsic right of the state to kill. Professor Rocchio envisages certain primitive societies whose only means of protecting themselves is killing the criminal. But this argument is fundamentally flawed. Many primitive societies mutilate the criminal. It prevents a killer from killing again, it is barbaric, but most people would agree that it is less serious than killing the person concerned. But Vatican II condemned mutilation.

There is the additional problem of torture. In the United States, hanging, lethal injection, electrocution and the gas chamber are all legal. On the question of cruelty and the death penalty, in a stinging dissenting opinion, Chief Justice Brennan included a graphic description of electrocution. He wrote, quoting from documentation: 'the force of the electric current is so powerful that the prisoner's eyeballs sometimes pop out on his cheeks, the prisoner often defecates, urinates and vomits blood and drool . . . sometimes the prisoner catches fire . . .' In 1990, when Florida killed Jesse Tapero, flames shot out from his head. Accounts of the smell of burning flesh, of a man breaking free in the gas chamber during his execution, all demonstrate that the death penalty is not only torture, but its inevitability is, for the individual on death row, a recurring nightmare, an ongoing mental and psychological torture, a fact noted by the European Court of Human Rights. But Vatican II[12] condemned as 'infamies . . . which poison human society and . . . are a supreme dishonour to the Creator whatever violates the integrity of the human person, such as mutilation, torments inflicted on body or mind', etc. Surely the latter refers to torture. So Vatican II condemns punishments less serious than the killing which the Catechism upholds. The same Catechism also teaches that masturbation (2352) and fornication (2353) are gravely sinful, that all artificial control of reproduction by a married couple is intrinsically evil (2370), yet the deliberate killing of a criminal by the state is not. To make this comparison is to address the issues of consistency and credibility in the church's teaching.

Conclusion. The traditional benign church assumptions in regard to the state, to whom is conceded the right to kill its own citizens, seem archaic and irrelevant in the light of what has been documented here, i.e. the deadly combination of poverty, racism, guns, the susceptibility of an elected judiciary system to right-wing political and economic pressure in a punishment-orientated society, resulting in a loss of respect for human dignity, so that incarceration and killing are seen as the panaceas for all societal ills. This lethal combination has led the Bishops of Texas (1997) to say: 'the Catholic Bishops of the United States have repeatedly condemned its (the death penalty's) use as a violation of the sanctity of human life . . . we are deeply concerned that the State of Texas is usurping the sovereign dominion of God over human life by employing capital punishment for heinous crimes'. Not surprisingly, their condemnation was met with apathy and indifference, including by many Catholics.

Notes

1. *Statistical Abstract of the United States*, 1997, no. 363.
2. Joseph A. Califano Jr, 'A Punishment-Only Prison Policy', *America* 178.5.
3. Stephen B. Bright, 'Capital Punishment on the Twenty-fifth Anniversary of Furman v. Georgia', 26 June 1997.
4. Stephen B. Bright, National Public Radio Broadcast, June 1998.
5. Professor Weidner, lecture at St Mary's University, San Antonio 1995.
6. James J. Megivern, *The Death Penalty*, Mahwah NJ, 19ff.
7. J. N. D. Kelly, The *Oxford Dictionary of Popes*, Oxford 1986.
8. Peter de Rosa, *Vicars of Christ*.
9. Megivern, *The Death Penalty* (n. 6).
10. *Catechism of the Catholic Church*, London 1994, no. 2266.
11. Professor Vincent Rocchio, 'The Ultimate Litmus Test', *National Catholic Register*, 7–13 December 1997.
12. Vatican II, *De Ecclesia in Mundo Huius Temporis*, no. 27.

A Carefully Hidden Reality

Enrico Chiavacci

I

The globalization of human life on the planet is an irreversible fact. But it is also a recent development, no more than fifteen to twenty years old: it is a development which came about with the silicon revolution and the technological consequences which that has for communication and transport. The mere fact that all humankind no longer appears as a simple sum total of sovereign states (or of cultures, religions, races, etc.) but as a single social body united by a common destiny is theologically relevant in a positive sense: it is a decisive transition in the history of humankind on its way towards the goal willed by God. The specific and inescapable mission of the church is to animate the human 'family' so that it becomes the 'family of God' (*Gaudium et spes* 40). The theme of the human family as a unity and of the growing awareness of such unity is explicit in *Gaudium et spes* 77, and the vocation which is 'both human and divine' to build up the world in true peace is now understood as the common responsibility of all human beings towards the human family (*Gaudium et spes* 92). This responsibility certainly holds for present-day humankind, but also for future generations: it is a responsibility towards the history of a human family which is always on the way to the fullness of the kingdom. That constitutes a theological basis for preoccupations with ecology (not the only one, but certainly the most important one).

The importance of the process of globalization is largely understood in today's church (with some resistance from the authorities) and among all men and women of good will. What, however, is not understood is the mechanism which today gives rise to the process of globalization and dominates it. The first thing to understand is that any form of relationship between human beings is mediated by structures: this is true in every case, in immediate relations between individuals (in which the main structure is language) and above all in relations between individuals or groups which do not have direct and immediate contact. Globalization is possible only by means of extremely complex planetary structures which have to cover all the geographical areas and all the fields of interaction (political, economic, cultural, etc.) which are relevant to human society.

Today the only fully effective planetary structures are those of the economy and of mass communication, and as we shall see, the latter is almost totally dependent on the former. The economic structure is in reality a complex system of structures which *de facto* dominate the whole of economic life on the planet, above the heads of individual states and governments, however powerful these may be. The process of globalization is dominated by economic reality. We shall consider four elements which define what is called 'economic reality' today.

II

The first element is production. Today anyone can produce wherever it is convenient and possible to produce: the most important factor here is the cost of labour, and perhaps above all the availability of qualified labour and adequate plants and infrastructures. Moreover nowadays the more complex products are manufactured component by component, and each component is produced wherever is possible and convenient. A very simple video-cassette has the plastic parts produced in countries with a largely unskilled labour force; the tape in a country with a better qualified labour force; the assembly takes place in a third country and the marketing in a fourth country (a typical sequence might be: Thailand, Japan, Taiwan, France). But an aeroplane can be composed of 172,000 parts (information from Airbus), each of them produced in different places by different firms, whereas only three firms in the world are capable of producing the engines (two in the USA, General Electrics and Pratt and Whitney; and one in the UK, Rolls-Royce).

The second element is distribution, which in practice means the market. Today the computer allows one to know the catalogues, the costs, the availability and the demand of goods in real time all over the world. New transport technologies – trains with a capacity of more than 10,000 tonnes and ships carrying 7,000 containers [1] – make the unit cost of goods transported negligible. We have a single planetary market: without exception, all the goods of a state or an area are conditioned by this market and can only survive within it.

The third element, new in respect of the economic theories which are now dominant, is the importance of the phase of research and development. It can be fifteen years from the first idea for a new plane to the beginning of mass production; the latest generation of locomotives have taken twelve years to develop and are still not satisfactory; biomedical research is very slow by nature, very costly and concentrated in a few specialized laboratories.[2] The result is that today enormous amounts of capital have to be invested not only in production but also in new research: in the market the competition between big businesses translates into a desperate search for novelty.

The fourth – and most important – element is the advent of a world financial system and a world financial market. The new technologies of communication allow the movement in real time of enormous amounts of capital from one end of the world to the other, without any possibility of control or even simple monitoring of this movement by states or governments. All money, however and wherever on earth it is collected (banks, credit institutions, shares, bonds, etc), comes to centres which trade capital; these in turn are controlled by big transnational financial businesses, often without a name. That also happens with currencies: a big financial firm can make a currency collapse, and thus put pressure on a country, ruining it or forcing it to adopt an economic policy which is more convenient for the financial company that controls its investments (this is probably one of the reasons for the recent financial crisis in Asia).

According to credible surveys, every day between three and ten trillion dollars are moved across the face of the earth: they move in real time, uncontrollable, and they always move in the direction of the maximization of the private profit of capital. An investment business does not make a profit from production but from the movement of capital. We need to understand clearly that today finance and production are completely separate. Investment businesses are not interested in what is produced, in what quantities and by whom: they are interested only in maximizing the expectation of short-term profit (the variations between shares on the stock market – the only thing that an investment business is interested in – is usually calculated on a quarterly basis, but often it is invested for between twelve and twenty-four hours). Whether to invest in arms or medicine, in drugs or schools, in commodities which pollute or which do not pollute, which create jobs or destroy them, are meaningless questions for the anonymous figures who run the world capital. Any concern to invest in the goods necessary to satisfy the most urgent needs of the poor of the earth is completely alien to capital. On the contrary, it can be in its interest to invest in the production of commodities which serve no purpose or which are even harmful: in the classic theory there may not be a demand in the market for such goods, but today demand is created through the media. It is important to understand that there are 'induced needs', i.e. there is a demand for things which serve no purpose but which when put on sale offer large profits. The function of the media is an essential part of the planetary economic system, but the media require enormous amounts of capital which are controlled by the same centres that control marketing and production.

Thus a large part of the needs of the poor of the earth – now around eighty per cent of humankind – cannot become a demand in the planetary market because of a lack of money (as we have seen, demand on the market can be not only induced but also repressed: and it is called a free market!). The goods capable of satisfying such needs have a prohibitive cost for the poor, because they are determined by the chain of maximizing profit and not by the costs of production. If an industry or even a corporation does not maximize profit, its shares and its financial credibility collapse, and in a chain reaction the credibility of the banks which have rashly provided credit for it also collapses, with further consequences along a chain which we cannot discuss here.

III

This situation determines a condition of equilibrium on the planetary market of goods and capital which can be described like this:[3]
– The rich area of the planet has a disposable wealth per year and per head (GNP) of between $20,000 and $30,000; Latin America, South Africa and some (a few) countries of South East Asia of between $1500 and $5000; the whole of central Africa and a large part of Asia of $100 to $600. The availability of wealth per head in the second area is a tenth of that of the rich area and that of the third area one hundredth.
– Child mortality – in the first year of life per 1000 live births – is 6 in the rich area, between 30 and 60 in the second area, and between 60 and 120 in the third area. Exceptions worth noting are Cuba, which has a European average, and Vietnam, with 35 as compared with Cambodia, which has the same wretched GNP of $260 but a child mortality of 105. These figures relate tragically to the availability of food, of drinking water, of medical aid, of living conditions, and of the level of education for the vast majority of the human family. An anti-abortionist who is also a convinced supporter of free trade – a frequent combination today – is either a schizophrenic or is totally misinformed.
– In the rich area life expectancy is around seventy-seven, in the second area between sixty and seventy, and in the third area between forty and sixty. In almost all the countries in sub-Saharan Africa the average life expectancy is below fifty.

These are average figures which have an indicative value; but they are true figures in the sense that almost all countries come within the fluctuations indicated above, and they are figures which allow useful and sorry comparisons. This situation is a static one: from the report of the Brandt Commission (1980) to the present day relations have not changed in the poorest countries except for the worse. So the situation does not depend on the good will of this or that government or economic operator: it is maintained by the planetary economic system which is dominant today. Its profound logic, derived from the idea of the free market, is the maximization of private profit both at the level of finance and at the level of productive enterprise. In this logic the very idea of a common good of the human family is completely meaningless, as are the human rights listed in the 1948 United Nations Declaration of Human Rights.

I do not believe that the majority of the inhabitants of the rich area of the planet are heartless or without human feelings, rejecting the idea of brotherly solidarity in respect of fundamental human rights. But if that is the case, we have to ask how this situation is being maintained, and why it is thought to be either natural or at least as irreversible and fated as the movements of the stars. We must ask how there is no international agency with the task and the authority to change the situation. Even the threads of the situation are in private hands, without any public authority. A broad popular consensus in the rich countries could pressurize their respective governments to work jointly to modify the system of structures which govern almost all the planetary economy. Hence there is a need for those who hold economic power to hide the tragic reality of the global condition of the human family by means of a system of lies, disinformation, induced mentalities. And this need for lies and disinformation extends to the ecological situation. Whatever the means proposed to deal with the situation, they are always treated as costs which reduce the short-term or medium-term profit. The most authoritative publications on economics see the ecological problem as a problem of the cost/benefit relationship, and not as a problem of the quality or of the survival of human life on earth.[4] Lies or disinformation, whether on the economy or on ecology, are produced by means of control of the media – TV, radio, the Internet, the press – which today are almost completely in private hands. However, here we touch on another subject. I now want to examine some operations, all of which are substantially mendacious.

A first lie is the hidden virtue of the free market. For classic economics, the free market is one in which sellers and buyers find a price equilibrium which is the best compromise between opposing requirements. But the presupposition of all the great classics on economics was that no operator – buyer or seller – was strong enough to be able to modify single-handed the point of equilibrium, the price generated by the goods. Today this is a ridiculous notion: the disequilibria on the planetary market are tremendous. This is even more the case in the capital market, which the classic economists did not even think of. In a world market the poor will always be the losers. But the theme of the free market was later developed by John Stuart Mill towards the end of the eighteenth century: it is always a mistake to help the weakest. Total freedom favours those who produce or use wealth more efficiently and hence increase the global wealth of a country. The fate of the inevitable losers must be entrusted to private charity: this was already the case then and is attested by Karl Marx in the first book of *Das Kapital*, but also and more lastingly by Charles Dickens. Think of the description of the workhouses in *Oliver Twist* or of the new industrialized city in *Hard Times*. In a single planetary system the theorem of John Stuart Mill is inapplicable: today at least two-thirds of humanity would have to survive on the private beneficence of charitable institutions of a tiny minority of the rich. The economic experts know all this very well, but in almost all the media these experts always glorify the great benefits of the free market, whose 'invisible hand' will bring great benefits to all.

A second lie, connected with the first, is that if there are poor areas or countries, it is their fault. The origin of this idea lies in the Calvinistic matrix of white North American culture. It follows from the doctrine of predestination that only those who are blessed by God achieve economic prosperity. The affirmation of the richest is an indication of goodness: the one who is good is successful, and if someone is not successful it means that he is not good. This basic idea today (though this is not Calvin's fault) explains the desperate and obsessive search for wealth, for possessing more as the only goal in life, and the disparagement of poverty: in the WASP society of the United States all this is now an automatic criterion of judgment – which is accepted uncritically. However, it operates today throughout the rich West, simply assuming different appearances. The fault is said to lie with the governments of the poor states, which are incompetent or corrupt or closed to the idea of the free market. Now it is true that many governments are incompetent or corrupt, but that is also the case in the rich countries. And conversely it is true that in a poor country the room that a government has for manoeuvre is determined by its GNP: it is possible to direct the scarce resources in different ways, but the resources are always scarce. Above we have noted the contrast between Cambodia and Vietnam and between Brazil and Cuba. But the USA also has a GNP greater than that of the European Community, and all the indications of quality of life – average life expectancy, child mortality, health aid, literacy – are worse than those of the European countries. This happens in both poor and in rich countries: a better quality of life, wretched though that may still be, is connected with a social concern understood as a specific task of the government (the pursuit of the common good to the limits of the possible) and hence with the rejection of the free market as the supreme regulator of the economy. However, the IMF grants aid or renegotiates old debts only on two conditions: an increase in taxation or a squeeze on consumption. And these criteria are adopted by all the institutions disposed to invest in poor areas. But how does one squeeze the consumption of those who live on a third of a dollar a day? Sub-Saharan Africa is a special case: there is not even a minimum of primary literacy (secondary literacy is virtually non-existent); there is no infrastructure (energy, transport, etc.) and therefore it is quite unsuitable for any form of investment. Sub-Saharan Africa is almost non-existent for the planetary economic system: only a very few countries appear in the statistics on poor countries which are published every six months in the most important economic journal in the world, *The Economist*, and then only rarely. This is an area in which the economic operators are not interested and its destiny is entrusted almost exclusively to private beneficence.

Another form of this second lie, which is quite popular, is that the poor of the earth are poor because they are mentally inferior, or because they have not wanted to do anything. It is true that there is a minimum of primary literacy in the poor areas, at least in the cities. But this is because the schools are poor, unattractive and without suitable premises, in classes which can range between 50 and 100 pupils, who alternate every three hours, with teachers who are badly prepared and badly paid. The majority of children leave after two or three years; they will have to work hard because even their small contribution is necessary for the survival of the family. It is not rare for boys and girls to be sold into prostitution or slave labour so that the rest of the family can survive. And it is common for children to be stolen for adoption abroad or for organ transplantation: in the poor countries many children are not registered because registration costs money and requires impossible journeys, so that the parents cannot even report the theft of the children. But when the child is sent to a good free school, the results are surprising: I myself have been involved in such a programme in a *favela* in São Paulo, and all those who we have been able to get to university have passed the strict admission examination first time and have achieved good grades within the prescribed period. So much for the charge of inferior mentality. Again in São Paulo, all the youths of modest families who go to the university work all day and go to the university from seven in the evening until ten or eleven: so much for the accusation of reluctance or laziness.

At the state university of Phnom-Penh in Cambodia, at the request of a non-governmental organization I gave an upgrading course for professors of philosophy for one month: I lectured for fifty-four hours between two and five in the afternoon, at a temperature of 37° and without air-conditioning, because the professors had to lecture to the students all the morning. What Western professor would work in the faculty from eight in the morning until five in the afternoon, non-stop and in such climatic conditions? At the end I examined the professors and found them competent to take academic degrees in any important faculty (Hong Kong or Singapore), but at the time neither they nor the state had the necessary funds. Here we need to ask what cultural wealth, what scientific capacity, is being lost on earth. We also need to ask how much falsehood and how much disinformation dominates – deliberately – the populations of the rich countries.

A third lie is that in the poor countries the cost of living is much lower than in the rich countries. It is a lie which has also been made official in many statistics; instead of the GNP these indicate the PPP – purchase parity power, a GNP adjusted to the cost of living on the basis of a basket of goods. On the technical level this new index has little to do with PNL and is thus to be regarded as a trick. On the practical level some simple goods – an egg, a chicken, a reel of cotton – are pretty cheap; but any kind of more complex goods has a price comparable to our own, and often higher than our own (books, hygienic products, irons, refrigerators or poor-quality washing machines). The families survive, when they do, without homes: living in huts they make themselves, with no heating whatsoever, buying second-hand clothing, walking many kilometres on foot to get to work,[5] opening little stalls on the roadside in the open or in wretched shelters.

The vast tragedy in which the great majority of the human family survives is carefully concealed. It is known that there is famine in the world, that it is good to send some goods or used clothing to the poor. However, the fundamental fact that this is a stable, structural condition, beyond any possible definition of a dignified human life, is kept hidden. The condition in which the great majority of the human family lives is one of desperation or passive resignation, of a loss of any kind of hope or horizon of life except that of 'what shall we have to eat tomorrow?'[6] And when during courses or conferences I try to explain and denounce such a reality I often find myself confronted with an unwillingness to accept what I say, based on the lies that I have described above. And these are lies and disinformation provided by the media.

The tragic planetary structural triad – economy–ecology–media – cannot be accepted by a Christian conscience either out of conviction or out of resignation. We have to react to it, either denouncing it or seeking alternative forms for the future of globalization. Neither the church nor the local churches can remain neutral, above the parties, when confronted with cultural and political imperatives which tend to maintain or to combat this tragedy.

Translated by John Bowden

Notes

1. 'Heavy Haul Horizon', *Railway Gazette International* 154.2, February 1998, 91–106; L. Bromberger, 'Inévitable Anvers', *La vie du rail et des transports*, no. 2674, 9 December 1998, 52–9.
2. *The Economist*, 'A Survey of the Pharmaceutical Industry', 21 February 1998, 3–18.
3. The statistics given here are taken from Britannica World Data, *Encyclopedia Britannica Yearbook 1998*; United Nations Development Programme, *Human Development Report* 1997, Oxford 1997 (in which A. Sen has played a key role); *The Economist, World in Figures 1999,* London 1998.
4. There is an interesting and perceptive comparative study of this double approach to the ecological problem in *The Economist*, 'A Survey of Development and the Environment. Dirt Poor', 21 March 1998, 3–16. The final paragraph is illuminating. It concludes: 'People might start to assume, wrongly, that capitalism and foul living conditions are natural bedfellows, just as Engels did last century', which should be avoided at all costs. There is a very acute analysis, in connection with the Kyoto conference on the environment, by W. K. Stevens, 'National Interests Clash on Averting Global Warming', *International Herald Tribune*, 1 December 1997.
5. In São Paulo, Brazil, the bus costs one dollar. On the edges of the city it is often necessary to take two buses to get to work. Four dollars a day on a medium to low salary of 400 dollars a month is unsustainable.
6. The analyses by J. K. Galbraith, *The Nature of Mass Poverty*, London 1979, are still very important, as I have been able to verify in many areas.

Sin of the World, Light of the World

José-Ignacio González Faus

> The modern world is full of Christian ideas that have gone mad (Georges Bernanos)
>
> God is angry, God is absolutely furious at what is being done to the people of South Africa today. I say this without any hesitation (Albert Nolan in 1987)

Following Karl Barth's venerable advice ('the Bible in one hand and a newspaper in the other'), one would have to try to read scripture with one eye on the biblical text (here the two phrases from John) and the other on the text of life that is taking shape in culture and social institutions. Only thus can reading of the Word avoid the blurred focus of a one-sided abstraction, which can no longer be challenging since it has eliminated all concretions.

So I hope I can stick to the set subject (a biblical-theological analysis of the Johannine notion of 'sin of the world') through letting this analysis bring me constantly to references and allusions to our world. To exemplify these allusions, let us see how differently many phrases from the Fourth Gospel sound if we replace the abstract word world with such historical embodiments as our progress, or our longing for freedom, which at present structure our world.

I. Sin of the world, sin of progress

Two observations suggest that this is justifiable substitution:

1. All progress seeks to be in effect a step from chaos to cosmos, to the already ordered and adorned. World and progress therefore have a certain relationship, though they are not equivalent. They become more nearly so if we allow that God does not create a static and finished world but that 'God wanted a world that continues to form itself and that, moreover, goes on forming itself largely through different initiatives'.[1]

2. Furthermore, progress can have (and does have) the same ambivalence as the term 'world' in the Fourth Gospel. As we know, the world is at once the object of the love of God, who sends his Son not to

condemn it but so that it may be saved by him (cf. 3.15, 17 and 12.45) and the object of God's condemnation, on whose behalf not even Jesus will pray (17.9), since 'its works are evil' (7.7). And these so opposed meanings sometimes coincide in expressions where it seems impossible to distinguish whether they refer to the first or the second, such as 8.26 when Jesus 'declare[s] to the world' or 11.27, where he is said to be 'coming into the world'.

On the basis of these observations, we can paraphrase the Fourth Gospel, replacing 'world' with 'progress' or 'freedom':

(*a*) 'Here is the Lamb of God, who takes away the sin of progress' (cf. 1.29);

(*b*) 'He was in freedom, and freedom came into being through him; yet freedom did not know him' (cf. 1.10);

(*c*) 'My kingdom is not from *this* progress' (cf. 18.36), or 'I am not of *this* freedom' (cf. 8.36);

(*d*) and next to these negative connotations for 'our' progress, we can place all the positive expressions in which following Jesus consists in recognizing him as 'saviour of freedom' (cf. 4.42), as 'the prophet who is to come into *this* progress' (cf. 6.14), or those in which Jesus describes himself as 'light of progress' or the one who gives light to progress (cf. 12.43; 6.34).

These are not nonsensical paraphrases. Progress and freedom are the great absolutes of our world – as motives of pride for the First World and as irresistible lures to the Third. But *this* progress that is 'ours' and with which we are arriving at the doors of 2000 is marked by a deep structural sin. And I believe that we Christians should bring to the turn of the millennium not only a mysticism to found progress and freedom but also a deep critique of many aspects (political, religious, cultural and economic) of *this* actual progress on which we are embarked – stressing the adjective 'this' in parallel with the times the Fourth Gospel links its critique to 'this' world (as in 18.36 cited above).[2]

To conclude this section: there exists a 'sin of progress', just as for the Fourth Gospel there existed a 'sin of the world'. We now need to ask what this sin is that Jesus unmasks and what this salvation is that he seems to offer the world. I shall come to this later in a more sociological analysis, summing up critiques of our progress under three headings: the reasoning it uses, its lack of solidarity, and its incapacity to adopt the viewpoint of the victims it produces.[3] First I am going to try a similar critique, but from the theological viewpoint of the Fourth Gospel and what it says about 'this' world.

II. The plot of this world: lies and victims of violence

In various places John seems to view the sin of the world as an order built on an implanted lie that encourages murderous violence – or one built on murderous injustice that hides itself under lies. The Fourth Gospel is not far from Paul's celebrated definition of sin as 'oppressing the truth with injustice', though – contrary to Paul – it expresses this in more structural than personal terms. Let us look at some examples:

1. For Jesus, the world does not know God as Father and as Just (cf. 17.25). This is the root of all opposition between Jesus and the world, which we shall look at in the next section: God as Father is the foundation of a brother- and sisterhood from which no one, not a single person, can be excluded. And God as Just is, according to the whole biblical tradition, the vindicator of victims. Yet the excluded and victims are precisely the reverse of our progress.

2. When Jesus declares to Pilate that his kingdom is not from *this* world (18.36), the whole conversation revolves around these two points: if it was from this world, his followers would have defended him violently to prevent him from being handed over. And yet he has come into the world to testify to the truth. Pilate's reaction in breaking off the conversation can stand as a symbol of the reaction of our progress to truth.

3. Jesus defines the structuring principle (or 'the ruler', personified) of this world as a 'murderer' and 'the father of lies' (8.44).

4. Against these structuring principles – murderous violence and lies (or 'darkness') – Jesus appears constantly as the principle of life and of light (or truth: see 9.25 and 8.26, where Jesus tells the world what he has heard from 'one who . . . is true'). Light and life are the two themes already announced – together with rejection of the world – in that sort of musical overture, the Prologue to the Fourth Gospel.

If we then take a look at our world on the basis of these observations, it will not be difficult to give names to all those implanted falsifications and cover-ups for murderous violence that have woven the networks of inter-human relationships. For example:

(*a*) That falsification of the social fabric by which shared values (which are those that hold any true community together) have in fact become travestied interests. Nearly all our axiological words – country, freedom, religion, rights – nearly always cloak much uglier and less fraternal interests.

(*b*) That falsification of interpersonal relationships produced by what the Gospels call scandal (and we more simply call seduction, bad example, or mock desire) in which the offer of a way to fulfilment or happiness for another in fact masks the quest for confirmation of, or complicity in, one's own errant way – as with drugs or some forms of sexual seduction.

(c) The lie of induced 'false needs', presented as a new economic gospel, which degrades the supposed *homo sapiens* into a mere *homo consumptor*.[4] These are false needs, but they end up becoming so real that we have to plunder the planet in order to satisfy them.

(d) The lie of so-called 'industrial culture' (Adorno, Horkheimer), which perverts the fruits of the human spirit into simple objects of mass consumption – think of the majority of American films and television series.

(e) The lie of the so-called 'global market' as an ultimate, self-regulating, provident and integrating principle, which rejects all corrective mechanisms because it itself corrects its apparent(!) outrages simply on the basis of more market.

(f) The structural degradation of situations that require evil in order to survive, such as drug addicts who need heroin, or exploited children who cannot suddenly stop working because that would make things worse for them.

(g) Finally, the tremendous seduction of evil as a means of doing good, of wanting to do away with good on the basis of more evil. This is Girard's thesis of the sacralizing of violence as a means of putting an end to violence, when in reality this evil taken up as a means of salvation does no more than damage us and in the end brings out the worst in us.[5]

These examples are inevitably simplified, and reality is far more complex, furrowed with limit-situations which would require extensive qualification of the above statements and which are often the inevitable end point of a long previous history. But it should be clear that a world (and a progress) structured on the lie that ignores the victims in effect neither knows the God of Jesus (the just Father) nor has anything to do with Jesus' category of the reign of God.

The sin of the world can therefore be defined as a loss of light: human progress walks in darkness – in that 'darkness' that the Prologue to the Fourth Gospel (1.5) makes into a global mystery within which the later plot of the Gospel unfolds. The world is not advancing towards greater humanity despite its dazzling technological achievements, but seems to be moving towards the subhumanity of some (those excluded by this so far from global globalization) and the inhumanity of others (those who benefit from it).

But this loss of humanity by the North, which suffers from the progress of our world, is, to a large extent, the work of humankind, not some sort of fatality thrust upon us: the negative balance has come about because the light came into this world 'and people loved darkness rather than light' (3.19).

To sum up: the sin of the world is as if the world has been steeped in lies, a constitution or structuration through falsity, which – naturally – conditions people by steering them badly, but which they themselves started. The result is that this world 'cannot receive' 'the Spirit of truth' (14.17–19) and cannot give peace like that of Jesus (14.27).

III. Jesus: unmasking to conflict and love 'to the end' (13.1)

M. Kähler made famous the saying that the Gospels are narratives of the passion with a rather long prologue. Although this referred to the Synoptics, it is true of the Fourth Gospel as well, except that here the Prologue is not woven in through a fabric of historical episodes but through an ideological or theological one. What kills Jesus is an entrenched sin, a sort of spiritual cancer whose principles are – as we have seen – falsehood and violence. To these two terms, the Fourth Gospel constantly opposes two other principles that stem from Jesus (not from the *archon* or this world): light and love. Light stands up to lies, blindness and the darkness of pseudo-justifications,[7] while love creates a new atmosphere that changes people. Both principles take flesh in Jesus, whose words are true because they come from God (e.g. 17.8) and whose works are life because they are works of the Father (10.25). Let us look at this process in more detail.

1. Jesus' word always unmasks the fact that the works of the world 'are evil' (7.7), as are the reasons that underpin them, because those who express them 'seek only their own glory' (7.18). Jesus unmasks this, even though doing so earns him hatred, because this history does not provide his *kairos*, his opportunity (7.6). But even so, his unmasking ends by introducing a principle of subversion into this present order: 'I came into this world for judgment so that those who do not see may see, and those who do see may become blind' (9.39). The climax of this unmasking process is the sentence that concludes the episode of the man blind from birth, which is one of the most forceful in all four Gospels: 'If you were [really] blind, you would not have sin. But now that you say, "We see," your sin remains' (9.41).

2. Besides unmasking, however, Jesus offers people the chance of a change of belonging, the possibility of ceasing to be 'of this world' (8.23) and of becoming 'children of God' (1.12). This is not a matter of a mere change of name, or even of a new way of looking at things; this change is proved by the identification of disciples with Christ, which supposes a reconversion of human desire. Here two other very Johannine themes

come into play: bread and water. The 'bread from heaven' (6.32, 51) is contrasted with other bread that cannot avoid death or satisfy human longing for life (6.49, 50), and the living water with other water that fails to satisfy human thirst (4.13ff. and 7.37ff.).

3. As we saw at the beginning of this section, this belonging is revealed not only in Jesus' words but also in his works. Jesus not only denounces: he also acts. And what he does is inadmissible to the established order. He throws the merchants out of the Temple because the Name of God cannot be used for personal gain.[8] He saves the adulterous woman from being stoned because zeal for God's law cannot be used to condemn others but only to change oneself (8.33ff.). He heals on the sabbath because the world is accustomed to use what is most sacred as an excuse for turning its back on those it excludes . . .

These actions are a denunciation not only of personal attitudes but of social structures – because the world tends to institutionalize what it holds most sacred, making it an excuse for anti-fraternal oppression or personal profit. And – once more – to the extent that it is our 'Temple' or our 'sabbath' and the guarantee of our security as chosen ones, we could say that 'healing on the sabbath' would today equate with ignoring the harsh structural adjustments laid down by the IMF, which always fall most heavily on the same victims (but, again, who can ignore them without risking being forgotten and stoned, as I shall come to show later?). And expelling the merchants from the Temple could be denying what Baudrillard describes as 'the triumph of absolute merchandise', trying to suggest that maybe arms cannot be merchandise, that the human body cannot be merchandise, that human capacity for work cannot be market merchandise, and that money itself, which is the means of exchange, cannot be market merchandise.

4. Chapter 11 of the Fourth Gospel (46ff.) shows that all these actions, though Jesus sees them as his Father's works, constitute a threat to the 'established [dis]order' (Emmanual Mounier). So, at that frightened meeting of the Sanhedrin, the sin of the world begins to become clear, consisting in sacrificing however many innocents are needed to defend 'our holy place and our nation' (*topos kai ethnos*, 11.48). And the evangelist comments ironically on this, opposing the 'nation only' to the universal gathering of the children of God (11.52) and 'our' holy place to Jesus' laying down of his very life.

With this the virtually inevitable outcome is foretold. But before looking at this, a brief excursus is appropriate, pointing out what this means for Jesus' followers.

IV. Disciples like the Master: conflict in Christian life

The 'following' of Jesus is a Synoptic term that, in John, seems to be replaced by a sort of identification with Christ or an 'abiding' in him (15.4), which we can call discipleship. Its content is a life similar to that of Jesus, which will contradict the structuring principles of 'this order' without ceasing to love it – not being withdrawn from this world but being freed from its evil (17.11, 15). Disciples will find it hard to 'love their life' in a world such as this one (12.25). This supposes a final identification with the destiny of the Master: 'If the world hates you, be aware that it hated me before it hated you. If you belonged to the world, the world would love you as its own, [but] you do not belong to the world' (17.18, 19). This implies a contrast that is hard to bear: 'the world will rejoice; you will have pain' (16.20). Jesus, though, adds that this tribulation is vindicated by his victory over the world, which turns the disciples' pain into the birth pangs of a new world (16.20–22, 23). Here he seems to be taking up again the explanation he gave himself at a moment of spiritual tribulation (12.27): the difference between the grain of wheat that remains just a fruitless 'single grain' and that which 'falls into the earth and dies' (12.24, 25).

John demonstrates an almost fundamentalist simplicity in all this; today we would miss the other observation: a world that in spite of its sin is also taken up into Christ has also often hated disciples-in-name, precisely because they have not acted as disciples.[9] Nor does John recognize the existence of those who share in Christ outside the sociologically Christian body (Simone Weil, Gandhi . . .) who, with or without reference to Jesus, give lessons in discipleship to those we call Christian. But this simplicity in a situation so close to the origins can be forgiven.

V. The proof: either Christ or us (11.47ff.)

For the Fourth Gospel, the violent death of the one who was, at one and the same time, the sign of progress and of freedom (the 'light of the world') and the life of the world forms God's greatest argument for proving the sin of this presumed 'order', of this presumed 'progress' (*kosmos*). In my view, one of the values of the Fourth Gospel lies in the fact that, while few New Testament documents say more than it does about laying down one's life, it presents no linguistic ambiguity that would allow us to misunderstand this laying down as ontologically necessary to *placate* the wrath of a God whose justice has become incomprehensible. The death of Jesus does not give God 'satisfaction', at least not except in constituting God's supreme argument against 'this' world.

As ever, perception of this argument of God's is the work of the same Spirit of whom it is said that its coming to us will 'prove' (*elenchein*, 16.8) three things: the sin of the world; where righteousness then lies; and, consequently, judgment on this order:

(*a*) The sin consists in believing more in the values of this order or of this progress than in those Jesus represents ('they do not believe in me', 16.9). Jesus represents free giving and justice, universal belonging and solidarity. The values on which the world is based today could be qualified as efficacy above justice, the so-called 'gospel of consumption' above solidarity, and the technological imperative above belonging and free giving.[10]

(*b*) Righteousness consists in 'I am going to the Father' (16.10): that is, the one who reaches the true Goal of this order is Jesus, not the world. God's judgment proves Jesus' values right, not those of 'this' world. Therefore – according to John – the world is left with no choice but to believe and know that God has sent Jesus and loves those who live like him (17.21, 23).

For both these reasons, Jesus will go on to say that his 'kingdom is not from this world' (18.36). I have already said that this phrase does not have a temporal sense but an axiological one: the values that produce this (dis)order do not lead to the reign of God that Jesus announced. They are so alien to it that in the Fourth Gospel the phrase cited forms a sort of 'inclusion' with that in chapter 3 (vv. 3ff.): that in order to enter the kingdom of God people have to be born anew (to go from being children of this world to being children of God, as we have already seen). These two sole mentions of the word 'kingdom' define the whole discussion (the 'judgment', if you like) between Jesus and the Jews that runs alongside the account of what Jesus does in the Fourth Gospel.

(*c*) But the Spirit also, again for both reasons, proves the crisis of this order (or God's judgment on it), which consists in the atrocities it will have to accept in order to continue, by which the 'ruler of this world' is condemned from the moment he finds it necessary to eliminate the one who is precisely his light and his saviour: Jesus, the holy one of God. St Irenaeus was to say not long after this that the death of Jesus 'sums up the spilling of all the blood of the just and the prophets that has taken place since the beginning of history'.[11] This death sheds an unbearable light on all the victims on whom our progress is built, leaving it, like Lady Macbeth, obsessed by (but incapable of) washing the blood of its victims from its hands – whether these are the victims of an absolute market ruling everything (from the slave trade and the plunder of Latin America to the Third and Fourth Worlds that seem to be beyond our definition of 'world') or those who become victims through unmasking the lie of this order: Archbishop Romero, Martin Luther King, Ignacio Ellacuría, Juan Gerardi . . .

John anticipates this victory of Jesus to such an extent that he seems to forget its eschatological nature: he narrates a passion of a victorious and startlingly non-suffering Jesus, as has so often been said. But what has been said above should compensate for this eschatological anticipation. And in fact, after the Gospel, John's first letter explains this compensation: the victory that conquers the world is not only the death of Jesus (as suggested in 16.33) but 'our faith' (1 John 5.4). This faith already contains the option for a world and a progress that can make the values of human belonging to the divine and human solidarity its absolutes, in place of the values of total competitiveness, of the gospel of consumption and of the technological imperative.

This means that the kingdom being 'not from this world' still implies that it will show in numerous ways within history. One of its signs should be progress, provided that this is a progress in equality and not just in competitiveness; in solidarity, not in exclusion or enmity; in freedom and not in thousands of personal or institutional slaveries, even if this means a materially slower progress.

Small, pale, partial realizations of this form of progress flourish from time to time in various parts of the world. Then again: the 'Caiphas principle' seems to be overturned, and the witnesses who were taken out of circulation continue shedding new light and generating new life, like the grain of wheat that seemed to die in the ground.[12] Or again: there is that unstoppable protest that continues to resonate obstinately down the avenues of the global market and the 'end of history' – which I hope will go on resonating down the coming millennium.

VI. Conclusion: Dionysus and/or Crucified Christ?

The dilemma of this article can seldom have been formulated better, in my view, than by Nietzsche in one of the contrasts he drew between Dionysus and the Crucified Christ. As he so acutely notes, 'it is not a difference in relation to martyrdom but in the meaning attached to it'. And he formulates this thus:

> In the one case, life itself, its eternal fecundity and its eternal return produce torment, destruction, and the will to annihilate. In the other, the suffering of the Crucified Christ as innocent, as objection to this life, and as formula for his condemnation.[13]

The lucidity of the unbelieving Nietzsche can reach no further than this point. What followers of Jesus find themselves called to accept is that 'the innocence of the Crucified Christ that serves as argument' does so not in order to condemn the world but to save it (John 3.17): that the Crucified Christ can redeem Dionysus and regain 'life and its eternal fecundity' by freeing it from the will to annihilate.

This is the unique Christian challenge. It is not surprising that it should be rejected. But it also seems probable that the only hope for 2000 will be realized if the world is steered in this direction and not in the opposite – even though there is still a long way to go.

Translated by Paul Burns

Notes

1. X. Zubiri, *El problema teologal del hombre*, Madrid 1997, 197.
2. This structural sin is so radical and so basic that even Karl Marx could justify the annexation of California by the United States as being carried out in the name of progress. And he adds: 'Or is it a misfortune that the splendid California was seized from the lazy Mexicans who did not know what to do with it?' (cited in Various, *Lo santo y o sagrado*, Madrid 1993, 192).
3. Cf. Various, *El secuestro de la verdad*, Santander 1986, 149–56. Also 'El pecado estructural', ch. 5 of my *Proyecto de hermano. Visión creyente del hombre*, Santander ²1991.
4. See the commentary by J. Rifkin on E. Cowdrick, *The New Economic Gospel of Consumption*, 1927, and the changes of values it supposed, summed up by J. K. Galbraith as 'creating needs and striving to satisfy them': J. Rifkin, *El fin del trabajo*, Barcelona 1996, 42ff.
5. 'Provocators, tyrants, all those who in one way or another offend their neighbours, are guilty not only of the evil they commit but also of the perversion they bring to the spirit of the offended' (Manzoni, *I promessi sposi*).
6. Or judgment: since commentators generally agree that the Fourth Gospel takes the form of a trial in which no one accuses, but the guilty condemn themselves. Cf., e.g., O. Tuñi, *El testimonio del evangelio de Juan*, Salamanca 1983.
7. Curiously, the Fourth Gospel is full of apparently valid arguments for those who do not wish to believe in Jesus: his words are absurd (6.60); he does not keep the sabbath (9.16); none of the authorities have believed in him (7.48); he comes from Galilee and does not fulfil any of the scriptures (7.41) . . .
8. The 'Father's house' made into a 'market place' (2.16).
9. The recent theme of the church's petitions for forgiveness, which John Paul II – and John Paul I before him – have sought to bring to the fore.
10. The first two are self-explanatory. By 'technological imperative' I mean that sort of compulsion by which, if a thing is technologically possible, it has to be done and eventually is done – with no purpose beyond showing that it could be done, and without asking whether it is beneficial or harmful to God's favourites, the victims, or

to the ecosystem that makes up the world as creation, or to the human race (as in the case of human cloning, which now looks inevitable).

11. AH, V, 14, 1.
12. 'The very day they killed Mgr Romero was when I decided to become a priest', a young Salvadorean told me not long ago.
13. *Nachgelassene Fragmente 1888–1889*, in *Werke*, Berlin 1972, VIII/3, 58.

II · The Hope of the Jubilee in Religious Traditions

The Jubilee in Judaeo–Christian Tradition

Elsa Tamez

For Christians, one of the most significant aspects of the jubilee tradition in the Hebrew Bible is the fact that Jesus of Nazareth built on it in his proclamation of the kingdom of God. His practice of liberating and healing would have been understood at the time as measures guided by the background of the jubilee.

These are not just more or less accurate deductions, since they are made explicit, at least in Luke 4.18–19, where Jesus begins his ministry by taking up 'the year of the Lord's favour' in reading the words of the prophet Isaiah (61.1–2) referring to the jubilee. The core of the message refers to liberation, which will be 'good news to the poor'. He twice mentions freedom (*aphesis*[1]): 'release to the captives' and the oppressed 'go[ing] free'. Giving sight to the blind can be understood as freeing the blind from their prejudice, or people from their narrow understanding, or it could be read as releasing from prison (cf. Isa. 42.7).[2] Furthermore, the Greek word *aphesis*, freedom, is the same word that Septuagint employs for remission of debts (in Hebrew *shmittah*; cf. Deut. 15.1), which were generally linked to slavery. So there is no doubt of Luke's – or Jesus' – deliberate intention of putting the jubilee into effect with the arrival of Jesus.

To understand just how radical Jesus' words in Luke 4.18–19 were, we need to know the tradition of his Jewish people. So in this article I propose to analyse briefly the jubilee laws of the people of Israel within the specific context in which they arose. I shall also allude to their limitations as a structure on which to build a just society, and conclude with an updated meditation on Ezekiel 46 as an example that links utopian vision with a historical embodiment.

I. Jubilee texts and their context[3]

Mention of the jubilee generally makes most readers of the Bible think of Leviticus 25, which is a late reference included in the Holiness Code, worked out by priests during the exile or on the Israelites' return from exile (c. 583 BC). This is indeed a clear enough expression of the jubilee proposals. The focus of the text is on redistribution of land and return to one's own family – perhaps in the sense of ceasing to work as slaves for others. The jubilee year explicitly proclaims 'freedom'[4] for 'every one' of the inhabitants (Lev. 25.10, 13). This suggests that recovery of one's own piece of land means liberation, as does returning to one's own family.

Jubilee and liberation were practically synonymous in the eyes of their beneficiaries: these include the land itself, since in that year the land should not be worked either, since it coincides with the year of sabbath.[5] Leviticus 25.11 states: 'That fiftieth year shall be a jubilee for you: you shall not sow, or reap the aftergrowth, or harvest the unpruned vines. For it is a jubilee; it shall be holy to you: you shall eat only what the field itself produces.'

The law establishes the proclamation of the jubilee as something solemn and transcendental: every fifty years and with the ram's horn 'trumpet sounded loud' (Lev. 25.9).[6] Furthermore, this year, with the Day of Atonement duly proclaimed, is declared hallowed (25.10).

The theological foundation for recovering land in the jubilee year is God himself, as owner of the land. Land, then, is not sold in perpetuity (25.23).

Using the jubilee year as a point of reference, the law lays down certain measures related to possible redemption of one's plot of land before the jubilee year (25.24–28). Those who lost their land were usually peasants who had been forced to sell it on account of financial difficulties (25.25). The law lays down that these do not have to wait fifty years to recover it if they have a *goel*, a close relative, who can buy it back, or if they themselves can find sufficient means to do so (25.25–26). The same applies to people. The law lays down certain measures for those whose extreme poverty has obliged them to sell themselves – which was not rare: see Nehemiah 5. In Leviticus 25.39–42, the law is addressed to Hebrews who buy Hebrews. These should not be treated as slaves but should live in the houses of those who have bought them as guest or hired workers, and they will go back to their lands and family at the jubilee. If a poor Hebrew sells himself to a foreigner, he can be redeemed before the jubilee by a close relative, computing the amount due by the number of years remaining to the jubilee year (25.47–55). The theological foundation of this is similar to that applying to the land. Poor Hebrews who have sold themselves as slaves should be treated well and redeemed by their brethren, since they are the property of no one but God, who sets free from slavery, as he did in Egypt (25.38, 42, 55). Unfortunately, this particular law does not apply to poor men and women from surrounding nations bought as slaves, who are excluded from this good news of freedom (25.44–46).

The text is drawn up against the recent background of the experience of exile in Babylon. As it was the priests who formed themselves into leaders and took on the task of preserving the memory of the traditions and the law, a religious tone and interest inform the redaction of these jubilee laws. Nevertheless, the vision of an egalitarian society emerges clearly – at least as applied to the Jewish people. Recovery of one's own plot of land and the opportunity of returning to one's own family argue against absentee landlordship and division into owners and slaves. And as this is a public law addressed to the whole people at a specific time, the proposals argue for a new economic and social order, with equal opportunities for all the inhabitants. Whether they were ever put into practice or not is a different question.

Leviticus 25.2–7 refers to a much older tradition deriving from the Covenant Code (Exod. 21–23), which seems to have been redacted in the eighth century. This deals with the sabbatical year. Exodus 23.10–11 legislates for letting the land rest and lie fallow after working it for six years. The explicit intention of letting the land rest every seventh year is that 'the poor of your people may eat' what it produces on its own and 'the wild animals' may eat what they leave (23.11). The mandate makes clear that this includes vines and olives, the most profitable crops. Harold Reimer has suggested that this action attempts to break temporarily the cycle of exploitation of the land, and so that of workers on the land.[7]

The freeing of slaves also appears in the Covenant Code in Exod. 21.2–6, which seems to be the oldest law of manumission. The difference that strikes one is that in this law slaves are to be set free every seven years and not every fifty. In Leviticus 25 slaves could be redeemed earlier by some relative if he paid, but if they had no next of kin to do this, they had to wait till the coming of the next jubilee, which came round every fifty years.

These ancient laws are believed to have their roots in the time before the monarchy, in the period of a confederation of tribes guided by the liberator God. Or, as Ross Kinsler indicates, they would have formed part of the vision of those who were to initiate a different way of living, in a new land, after experiencing slavery in Egypt and wandering in the desert in search of this dream. Later, during the exile, the priests used the idea of jubilee to re-create this past socio-economic Israelite order.[8] In any case, the drawing up of the jubilee code would have been a response to the injustices committed by the rich against the poor, which they prophetically denounced.

Unfortunately, the law lacks equality in dealing with women slaves, since these could not enjoy its freedom: 'When a man sells his daughter as a slave, she shall not go out as the male slaves do' (Exod. 21.7). This gender distinction does not appear in the jubilee year, nor in the Deuteronomist's re-reading of the Covenant Code. The sabbath year also appears in the Deuteronomic Code (12.26), drawn up at the beginning of the seventh century, after the fall of Samaria, perhaps during the rule of Manasseh. It is thought that Joshua was to make use of these laws in his reforms.

This code deals not only with the freeing of slaves every seven years (15.12–15) but also with pardon or remission of debts. Deuteronomy 15.1 begins, 'Every seventh year you shall grant a remission of debts'. It is not surprising that debts and slavery are intimately related, since falling into debt was the main cause of becoming a slave, as we have seen above. Deuteronomy 15 is more explicit and more just than the jubilee year in Lev. 25.39–43, since men and women slaves – there is no gender distinction here, as there is in Exod. 21.7 – are set free because their debts are remitted; and not only this: measures are enjoined to prevent their future indebtedness and so possibly relapse into slavery, since the year of the sabbath here includes an indemnity for those set free, so that they have a chance to restart their lives as free persons.

In the jubilee year and the year of sabbath, rest or suspension of the exploitation of the land and those who work it is regulated. This has led some commentators to point to the sabbath, the seventh day of the week, devoted to rest, as the central element in a socially and economically just society. It is not merely a question of a tradition according to which one does nothing and dedicates the day of the Lord to going to a service of worship. According to Ched Myers, economic and social justice in the Bible is based on God's call to keep the sabbath.[9] He sees, for example, the account of manna in the desert as a lesson related to economic production, since besides resting on the seventh day, there is no space offered for some people to accumulate and concentrate goods. The manna is collected each day for six days in sufficient quantities to live on, not stored – as it would rot – except on the sixth day, when a double amount is gathered so that there is no need to collect on the seventh day (Exod. 16.22–30).[10]

The law of the sabbath finds its oldest expression in Exod. 34.21, belonging to the Yahwist tradition, drawn up in the tenth to ninth century BC. As Harold Reimer points out, it concerns interruption of work at the time of greatest demand for production.[11] Exodus 34.21 states this clearly: 'even in ploughing time and in harvest time you shall rest'. Later, the Decalogue in Exodus 20 and Deuteronomy 15 repeats this, all-inclusively: family, servants and animals. The Priestly tradition legitimates this on the basis of God's own work and rest in the process of creation (Gen. 2.2).

In the Covenant Code, the sabbath comes immediately after the sabbatical year (cf. Exod. 23.12). A jubilee year or a sabbatical year cannot be conceived without the regular interruption of the fruits of work and the rest people need, at least once a week.

II. Limitations and strengths of the jubilee laws

There is no doubt that the jubilee proposal, as well as the laws governing the year of sabbath and the day of rest, were intended to form a society with socio-economic relationships based on justice, a justice legitimated by God, who is described as liberator. The redistribution of land, the remission of debts, the freeing of slaves, and the resting of the land and those who work it had no other aim than this, in a situation that was in need of it.

Nevertheless, being laws promulgated from within historical and cultural developments, they always ran the risk of being manipulated or distorted. By the time of Jesus, for example, the meaning of the sabbath day had been completely stood on its head. Instead of being an interruption of work for the sake of people, it had become a burden threatening people's lives. Jesus denounces this in Mark 2.23–28. The laws also include limitations deriving from the particular culture. In the Covenant Code, for example, women cannot be set free. The same applies to foreigners in the Deuteronomic code and in the jubilee year in Leviticus. In the Deuteronomic tradition, the *ger*, the foreigner, is defended, along with widows and orphans, but only members of the community are mentioned in relation to the freeing of slaves in the sabbatical year (15.12), which does not appear to apply in the – older – Covenant Code.

The same law of the sabbatical year in Deuteronomy 15 finds it necessary to legislate against those who try to forget or manipulate the remission of debts because they believe they will lose their money if they lend to the poor at a time close to the date of remission. Deuteronomy 15.9 warns: 'Be careful that you do not entertain a mean thought, thinking, "The seventh year, the year of remission, is near".'

When we come to the jubilee in Leviticus 25, the situation is more ambiguous. On the one hand, freedom from slavery is proposed every fifty years in place of every seven, which is clearly less attractive for those in need of freedom. On the other hand, when the text is considered in its historical setting, it is seen to concentrate on the exiles, who were not the poorest in Israel when they went into exile. So it is not difficult to understand their desire to regain their lands on their return. It is also possible to think that the proposition of fifty years for the jubilee is precisely because they spent fifty years in exile (587–538). Nehemiah 5 relates the conflicts that arose on their return from exile and how he had to decree justice to prevent the poorest falling into slavery on account of debt.

Because of the limitations inherent in these codes, Sharon Ringe has proposed that the jubilee laws should be seen as 'a powerful metaphor rooted in a social proposition, which does not, however, remain there but overflows it as an imaginative possibility capable of changing the world'.[12] There is indeed a marked difference in language between Isaiah 61 (Third Isaiah) and Leviticus 25, but both texts are linked. The prophet uses a more universal language of liberation, with eschatological force, while Leviticus legislates for the details of this utopia. The prophetic tone of Isaiah invites people to dream and has the power to mobilize those in exile to return to their land. Leviticus provides the historical setting in which the dream can become reality: with all having their own plot of land to work.

III. Proclaiming the jubilee on the way

When we speak of jubilee today, we need to be conscious of the actual situation in which we live: debts, poverty, unemployment, violence, discrimination, exclusion, conflicts, misery, dehumanizing consumerism, the lethargy of the churches. The jubilee, in this context, is the good news that supposedly puts an end to this situation of suffering and dehumanization. It is, obviously, much more than a 'negotiation' between rich and poor, debtors and creditors, unemployed and bosses, violated and violators. If we speak of jubilee in generic terms only, injustice is covered over, and the jubilee loses its force and ceases to be jubilee. But the jubilee, as we know, is not just around the corner. The question for Christians today is how to speak of jubilee in times of vulnerable hopes.

In Leviticus 25, those who do not repay debts can be condemned to death. So what we need to take from it is the idea that there will come a moment of liberation and elimination of injustices. This is perhaps why the prophets found it necessary to speak of a law written in human hearts, so that we love our neighbour not because the law enjoins this but because we just do, out of pure grace. This would be a law shot through with grace. In Ezekiel there is a tense and intended combination of grace and law that seems to seek to resolve the problem.[13]

It might be said that Ezekiel, an exiled prophet prophesying in the twenty-fifth year of the exile, so half-way to the jubilee, sees the jubilee as a river. He is guided by someone who shows him how the water increases as it flows out of the house of God. It begins as a trickle; then the guide measures a thousand cubits and it is ankle-deep; a further thousand cubits and it is knee-deep; a further thousand, waist-deep; and then he would have to swim to cross it (47.1–6). Then they return along the bank, and the guide points out the river's wonderful properties. This is a river that flows into the Dead Sea, a place where there is no life. The waters that spring from under the threshold of God's house flow eastward, into the most desertified country, through Arabia and into the Dead Sea. At this moment the waters are transformed into living, fresh waters.

The most interesting point is that the account of the overflowing river, which is pure grace and uncontrolled, is placed in the middle of a series of precise measurements, preceding it and following it. The previous chapters, 40–46, give the plans and measurements of the future temple; then comes the river that overflows all measurements, followed by more exact measurements, but this time applied to legislation for agrarian reform, the egalitarian sharing of the lands among the tribes. These laws, perhaps 'drenched' by the river of God, surpass the Mosaic laws, since in Ezek. 47.13–48.35 foreigners or immigrants are not only respected as stipulated by the law but also have the same rights to land as members of the community.

So, then, the dream will always be a dream, and this is how it should be: an open horizon inviting human beings to be beings worthy to reflect, ever better, creation in the image and likeness of God. This is our identity as humans from the theological point of view. But the dream on its own is not sufficient without plans, actions and actual laws aimed at bringing it about. Jesus took up the powerful jubilee discourse and put it into practice day by day through his actions. Both things are needed, and in tension with one another. And there, to the extent that we feel near this horizon, even in little things, the jubilee is coming about, God's grace is making itself felt, and the waters of the river are refreshing us, pleasantly.

Translated by Paul Burns

Notes

1. From the verb *aphiemi*, to make go, to let go, to allow, to loose, to pardon.
2. Cf. Sharon Ringe, *Jesús, la liberación y el jubileo bíblico*, San José 1997, 55.
3. I am using the text of the Hebrew Bible and insights from Harold Reimer, 'Leis dos tempos jubilares na Bíblia. Ensaio de uma perspectiva histórica', *Estudos Bíblicos* 58, 1998; Merlene and Frank Crüsemann, 'O ano que agrada a Deus', ibid.; Ringe, *Jesús* (n. 2); Jeffery A. Fager, *Land Tenure and the Biblical Jubilee*, Sheffield 1993; Jeffries M. Hamilton, *Social Justice and Deuteronomy. The Case of Deuteronomy 15*, Atlanta 1992.
4. In Hebrew *dror*, the term also used by Isaiah in 61.2 and by several kings of surrounding areas when they decreed acts of justice and liberation similar to the jubilee.
5. Cf. Lev. 25.2–7; Exod. 23.10–11; Deut. 15.
6. *jobel* (ram's horn) is the Hebrew word translated as 'jubilee', and most biblical scholars agree that the term derives precisely from this horn.
7. Reimer, 'Leis dos tempos' (n. 3), 23.
8. *The Biblical Jubilee and the Struggle for Life*, unpublished.
9. Ched Myers, 'Jesus – New Economy of Grace. The Biblical Vision of Sabbath Economics', in *Sojourners*, May–June 1998, 26.
10. Ibid., 26.
11. Reimer, 'Leis dos tempos' (n. 3), 19.
12. Ringe, *Jesús* (n. 2), 14.
13. Jon Douglas Levenson, *Theology of the Program of Restoration, Ez. 40–48*, Harvard 1975, 38ff.

Jubilee 2000 in the Teaching of John Paul II

David N. Power

With the approach of the third millennium, many people rejoice in humanity's technological and social advances and predict an ever more brilliant future. On the other hand, some are struck by the evils which the world is going to carry over the threshold of the century and see the dawn of the millennium as the prime time of the struggle between light and darkness. Millenarist and apocalyptic discourse can be given focussed expression in the prophecies and practices of cults. To avoid such misapprehensions, Christians need to find in their faith a way to express the balance between awareness of the reality of evil and suffering under which the world labours and the hope which the jubilee of the year 2000 may bring.

Convocation to jubilee

In his convocation to the celebration of the jubilee of the year 2000[1] and in letters and addresses preparing the church for that event, Pope John Paul II has done much to assess the sombre reality of the times in which we live, while issuing a strong call to hope in the name of the memory and the gospel of the Incarnate Word. The call which he has sent out is addressed of course primarily to the Catholic Church and is a call to an invigoration of its faith in Jesus Christ. A call, however, is also addressed to the world community of peoples to join in a common sense of reborn responsibility and to develop a hope that can be shared as a source of vital energy in rectifying injustices, in building a newly sensitive ethic, and in serving the needs of those who suffer the greatest burden of evil in our time.

Starting with the apostolic letter *Tertio Millennio Adveniente*, we find an address to the church and to the world community on how this jubilee, both religious and secular, should be prepared and celebrated. Indeed, Pope John Paul has called 'preparing for the year 2000' the 'hermeneutical key of my pontificate' (TMA 23). This concern for the advent of the new millennium has inspired the Pope himself in the choices of his papacy and offers those who would wish to understand his ministry a key to their interpretation. It is on the sense of reality and on the sense of hope invoked in his words that this article would like to focus, for this can contribute to a wider preparation for the start of a new millennium.

In calling preparation for the millennium the hermeneutical key of his pontificate, John Paul does so in a context wherein he records the efforts of the popes of this century to withstand totalitarian systems, to work for peace and to develop a social teaching adequate to the needs of humanity (TMA 22). This itself indicates both the range of the Pope's concerns and the desire to commune with all peoples in addressing the ills of the time, with hope. Most certainly his words are addressed primarily to the church in a call to a deeper conversion to Jesus Christ and faith in him, but his message goes beyond ecclesial boundaries to address persons of other religions and the community of nations on this 'time of choosing'.

The reference to this period of jubilee as a 'time of choosing' is a reminder of the words of Deut 30.15–19, with their resounding conclusion: 'Choose life so that you and your descendants may live, loving the Lord your God, obeying him and holding fast to him.' John Paul himself invokes the Old Testament texts on jubilee, to underline the foundation of a biblical legislation which is marked by the desire to bring emancipation to all who stand in need of being freed (TMA 12). With this in mind, he brings to the fore the words of Jesus when he proclaimed a year of the Lord's favour in the synagogue of Nazareth at the beginning of his ministry (TMA 11). In this connection, the Pope underlines the care of the poor and the search for a justice which respects all persons and their needs. Hence he finds it imperative that at this time the church should be mindful of its 'preferential option for the poor and the outcast' (TMA 51) and that it should find ways in which to engage peoples and nations in the quest for an era of greater peace and justice, on a global level. In a particular way in addresses for New Year and for the World Day of Peace, and in the Bull *Incarnationis Mysterium*, he has pointed to the international debt that weighs on some nations and calls for an exercise of international responsibility in the face of this burden.[2] Along with this, the Pope calls on all people, and especially on diplomats and politicians, to work for the cessation of violence which disrupts many peoples, nations and regions, and to a concern for the refugee and the outcast.[3]

The call to repentance

With a stark sense of reality, the Pope has repeatedly called attention to the miseries and tragedies peculiar to our modern times. There is the immense suffering of many, even of whole peoples. It is not by pure accident that the Holy See chose to address the question of the remembrance of the Shoah during this period of preparation for the jubilee and to enter into conversation with the Jewish people in addressing the church's responsibility in this catastrophe, as well as its responsibility to tend its memory in a way that serves its victims and prevents future tragedy. The naming of other tragedies in the thought of John Paul continues right up to the perils faced by the Islamic peoples in the Balkans at the end of the century.[4] In all of this, peoples and nations, and first and foremost the church itself, are called upon to make an examination of conscience and to seek a repentance which bears fruit in inner conversion and in just action.

The Pope looks for the roots of violence and injustice, in the persuasion that this is needed for the sake of engendering healing and hope. In particular, Christians and the followers of other religions that profess belief in the one God are invited to ask themselves how far they have lived and acted outside that faith. For humanity as a whole, John Paul points to a 'widespread loss of the transcendent sense of human life', a point to which he returns in the encyclical letter *Fides et Ratio*.[5] It is especially this which leads to disregard for the human person, he believes, and so to inhuman patterns of behaviour in the treatment of others.

> The general call to repentance addressed to the Church is formulated as follows . . . the Church should become more fully conscious of the sinfulness of her children, recalling all those times in history when they departed from the spirit of Christ and his Gospel and, instead of offering to the world the witness of a life inspired by the values of faith, indulged in ways of thinking and acting which were truly forms of counterwitness and scandal (TMA 33).

This is followed by attention to specific realities. The church is asked to repent for all that its members have contributed to the disunity of Christians, and for the acquiescence of its sons and daughters to intolerance and even violence. This repentance envisages not only the past, but also the sins whereby members of the church contribute to the evil of our own time. What the Pope notes is the contribution made by the lack of a deep faith to religious indifference, to the loss of the sense of human transcendence, and even to the violation of fundamental human rights. He links all of this with the failure to accept and integrate the teachings of the Second Vatican Council, an event of grace in our time to which we must seek an increasing openness.

Over a period of several years the Pope has spoken of several realities which are linked with this call to conversion.. They include the apologies given to the people of Africa and Latin America for the ways in which the church ignored and disregarded their cultures, the apologies offered to women for the ways in which they have been excluded from the life of the church, the inquiry into the history of the Inquisition, and most of all the repentant address to the memory of the affliction of the Jewish people in our century and in past centuries.

In addressing this need for an examination of conscience and repentance, Pope John Paul is accustomed to speak of the sins of the church's 'sons and daughters', while consistently affirming the holiness of the church itself as the bride and body of Christ. Some commentators ask whether the admission of fault does not have to go deeper and acknowledge fault and even sin on the part of the church as an institution and a living body, this aspect of its life, too, being touched by sin. No doubt this will continue to be debated, even as the lead is taken from the Pope in addressing the evils and sinfulness inherent to the church itself.

The Pope also issues an invitation to solidarity in repentance and conversion to those who are not members of the church. This is addressed in different ways to other Christian churches, to religions and peoples of faith in the One God, and to all who follow some form of religious belief and practice. It is also extended to all persons and communities who see the coming millennium as a time of jubilee in the sense that it is to bring about a renewal of human solidarity marked by the need to alleviate suffering and to give a greater share in the gains of human achievement to those who are left outside their compass.

The agenda for hope

The agenda which the Pope sets before us in taking this cognizance of the reality of evil and suffering can be summarized under four headings. There needs to be a purification of memories, a healing of memories, a memory of the 'new martyrs' and their witness, and a renewal of the pledge to serve the poor and the suffering. In this regard, he dubs the efforts to remember, to be obedient to the Spirit present in what is good in the movements and inspirations of the time, and the programmatic effort to bring peace and justice, a *prophetia futuri* such as was aroused in the time of the jubilee of the people of Israel in the biblical era (TMA 3).

The purification of memories is not meant to be a simple condemnation of past events and doings, least of all a pessimistic view of all that has come from modernity. In his encyclical on faith and reason, Pope John Paul is most careful to affirm modernity's primary contributions to the betterment of humanity. After reviewing the growing separation between faith and reason in the modern era, with the concomitant loss of the sense of the transcendent in human living, in *Fides et Ratio* 48 the Pope goes on to state:

> Yet closer scrutiny shows that even in the philosophical thinking of those who helped drive faith and reason apart there are found at times precious and seminal insights which, if pursued and developed with mind and heart rightly tuned, can lead to the discovery of truth's way. Such insights are found, for instance, in penetrating analyses of perception and experience, of the imaginary and the unconscious, of personhood and intersubjectivity, of freedom and values, of time and history. The theme of death as well can be for all thinkers an incisive appeal to seek within themselves the true meaning of their own life.

Here we see a capacity to sift through memories in a discerning way so that the 'purification' includes the power to affirm what is positive along with the awareness of what has been negative. Whether it is movements of thought or culture, or events and actions of the past, memory has to be able to perform this kind of discernment.

The healing of memories is more complex and more difficult, since it regards the divisions which peoples have experienced and most of the wounds inflicted on whole peoples or groups or races who have been victims of history. As Pope John Paul puts it, 'individuals and peoples need a sort of healing of memories, so that past evils will not come back again. This does not mean forgetting past events; it means re-examining them with a new attitude and learning precisely from the experience of suffering that only love can build up, whereas hatred produces devastation and ruin.'[6] This healing includes what has been said above about acknowledging wrongdoing and asking forgiveness. What the Pope hopes and expects to come from this is a new 'culture of peace'.[7]

When Pope John Paul mentions the memory of the 'new martyrs' of our era in writing of the millennium, he has in mind Christians, belonging indeed to different churches, who suffered for their fidelity to the faith in a time of ethnic persecution, racial hatred and totalitarianism. What is significant about them is that, in the name of Christ, they withstood even to death the evils against which Christians must stand in our time. As the martyrs of old testified to Christ in face of false claims and hatreds and so gave life to the church of their era, so the memory of these new martyrs can help to bring in a new advent of the reign of God in Christ (*Incarnationis Mysterium* 13). On some occasions in his papacy, for example in visiting the extermination camp at Mauthausen in 1988, this Pope has called on all victims of hatred, and especially the victims of the Shoah, to give their testimony to this age, speaking of their suffering and calling for conversion and change in the ways in which peoples deal with each other. This suggests an extension of the memory of Christian martyrs to embrace a larger memory. This will include the memory of persons of other faiths or persuasions who withstood evil with the shedding of their life-blood. Beyond that it must even include the memory of all victims of prejudice and hatred, asking them across time for the testimony of their anguish, lest it be forgotten. This is a hard and arduous cultural experience, but its neglect spells only disaster for the future.

The pledge to serve the poor and the suffering is the outcome of a public and culturally appropriate recording of these memories. It cannot remain a vague exercise of charity. It requires a systematic and co-operative approach to the redress of evil, undertaken by whole peoples under their religious, economic and political leadership. This is the part of the agenda for the millennium that the Pope presents most forcefully when he addresses those who hold public responsibility in these spheres. It amounts to a call for the forging of an international community, covering all fields of interaction, and built on principles of respect for human life and the dignity of persons.

Conclusion

Addressing the issues that lie before the international community for the year 1999, the Pope has stated:

> During this final year before the year 2000 an awakening of consciences is essential. Never before have the members of the international community had at their disposal a body of such precise and complete norms and conventions. What is lacking is the will to respect and apply them . . .[8]

This represents his effort to put before the international community of humankind, in terms accessible to all people, a vision of peace, justice and love. For him personally this springs from the faith that in Christ we are on a journey to God the Father. In the letter on the coming of the millennium, John Paul presents the vision of God the Father as one which must lead to a penance and a conversion which arises from trust in his love and from the faith that this love is offered to all. Others may not name human destiny in this way, but they can be invited to share the discernment of reality and the hope for peace which for Christians stems from this faith. Living from love, and only in living from love, it is possible to usher in the third millennium as an era of justice, peace and reconciliation between all who are divided, whether ethnically, racially, politically, economically or religiously. There is much for which to ask forgiveness in the human past but there is also much on which to build. This attention to reality, coupled with the quest for the foundations of hope, marks the approach to the millennium taken by Pope John Paul II in his address to the church and in his address to the nations.

Notes

1. John Paul II 'Tertio millennio adveniente. Epistula Apostolica anni MM Iubilaeum ad parandum', *AAS* LXXXVII, 1995, 5–41. English translation, 'The Coming Third Millennium', *The Pope Speaks. The Church Documents Bimonthly* 40, 1995/2, 85–113. Henceforth cited as TMA, with paragraph number.

2. See John Paul II, Bull of Indiction, *Incarnationis Mysterium* 12: 'Some nations, especially the poorer ones, are oppressed by a debt so huge that repayment is practically impossible. It is clear, therefore, that there can be no real progress without effective cooperation between the peoples of every language, race, nationality and religion. The abuses of power which result in some dominating others must stop: such abuses are sinful and unjust'. Latin original on internet, http://www.vatican.va/jubilee_2000. The translation is taken from *Origins* 28/26, 10 December 1998, 451.

3. See, for example, John Paul II, 'Issues before the International Community in 1999', Address to Diplomats, *Origins* 28, 31, 21 January 1999, 533–7. For a sense of a programmatic approach to the alleviation of human suffering, see 'Respect for human rights: the secret of true peace'. Message for World Peace Day 1999, *The Tablet*, 2 January 1999, 32–5.

4. See 'Issues before the International Community' (n.2.) and *Incarnationis Mysterium*.

5. See, for example, *Fides et Ratio*, 83. Latin original http://www.vatican.va/holy father. English translation, *Fides et Ratio. Encyclical Letter*, Boston 1998.

6. Pope John Paul II, 'Soltante tre anni. Ob diem ad pacem fovendam 1996 dicatum', *AAS* LXXXIX, 1997, 191–200. English translation, 'Offer Forgiveness, Receive Peace'. Message for the World Day of Peace (8 December 1996), *The Pope Speaks. The Church Documents Bimonthly* 42, 1997/3, 171.

7. Ibid.

8. 'Issues . . .' (n. 3), 4.

Asian Dreams and Christian Hope

Felix Wilfred

Joy and gaiety will mark the Christian celebration of the year 2000. The commemoration of this great occasion in the Asian continent should be such that it brings gladness not only to the tiny minority of Christians, but also to the three-fifths of humanity in this continent who are peoples of other religious traditions. In fact, as is well known, there are millions of Asians who, though they do not profess Christian faith and belong to an ecclesial institution, nevertheless nurse deep love for Jesus, are enamoured by his life and teaching, and even acknowledge the encounter of God with humanity in his person. Gandhi is the symbol of all those Asians who love and honour the memory of Jesus and let their lives be guided by his light and example.[1]

To celebrate the jubilee year with these Asian lovers and admirers of Jesus means that we take note of the fact that they too have their own ways of classifying time and marking calendars. While the Western calendar which computes the history from the birth of Jesus is used for secular purposes in Asia, the real cultural and religious life of the people revolves around local computation of time and calendars to be found in India and China and the various zones in South and East Asia under their civilizational influence. Calendars may refer to historical events such as the birth of Buddha, to the rule of emperors and kings, or may have society and its organization as the point of reference. For, 'temporal categories ("time-reckoning"), no less than the particulars of spatial classification, are products of culture and embody social meanings'.[2]

What has been said demands respect for the different cultural paths to time. Therefore, the celebration of the year 2000 may not rest on the triumphalistic assumption that this is the only chronology marking history.[3] The celebration of the year 2000 should not mean a *threat* to Asian peoples and their sense of history and time, but rather an invitation to celebrate joyfully the birth of Jesus whom Asia honours in its heart. Moreover, it is a significant occasion to reflect on how the Christian hope embodied in the person and message of Jesus could meet with the hopes of Asia and its many dreams – both in history and in contemporary times.

A thousand suns beyond the clouds

No people could survive without hope. Cynicism, despair and defeatism would have wiped them out from the face of the earth. If some of the ancient civilizations of Asia have survived uninterruptedly to this day, this fact cannot be explained without giving due credit to the element of hope that has been vigorously at work among them. This hope, nurtured through the culture and religious traditions, has flown into the Asian ethos, aesthetics, narratives and proverbs inspiring daily lives of the people. One such South Indian proverb says, 'There are certainly thousand suns beyond the clouds' – a proverb that provided the title to a fascinating book by the well-known French journalist Dominique La Pierre.[4] What is significant is that this hope – like the lotus flower – has found expression in Asia in the midst of adversities, amidst hopeless situations of poverty, malnutrition, misery and powerlessness.[5] This very situation has made the Asian masses a people of hope and resilience, dreaming for a new world and yearning for a different future.

Blossoms of hope

The dreams and hopes of Asia are expressed at different levels. To cite a few instances, in recent times we have witnessed how the hopes of the Indonesian people to have a just and democratic governance of their nation led to dramatic political changes in that country, thanks to the role the students played. In the Philippines, the long dictatorship of Marcos siphoning off the resources of the people (one has only to think of the 1700 pairs of shoes owned by Imelda Marcos!) was brought to an end without shedding a drop of blood, by the sheer confidence and hope of the people for a democratic future for their country. Most dramatic, however, was the way the courageous people of Vietnam withstood the most militarized power ever on earth and came out victorious. Struggles for democracy and human rights in Myanmar are waged today with indomitable courage under the leadership of the brave woman Aung San Suu Kyi.

Besides these significant events we have numerous peoples' movements in the Asian countries which are beacons of hope, and these relate to the issues of human rights, dignity and justice to women, protection of environment, and so on. These stories of hope are the antidote to demoralizing despondency and despair generated by powerlessness. In biblical terms, we in Asia are constantly in the situation of David confronting Goliath. The tribe of Davids in Asia is multiplying, and this is truly the strength of Asia for a future full of hope.

The mystery of hope

In the face of all this, we need to probe deeper into what appears to be a mystery lurking behind the dreams and hopes of people in Asia, and humanity at large. The myth of Sisyphus is the symbol of a human situation signifying the futility of even the best human struggles to conquer the inevitable. It is here that we realize the transcendent, or better trans-rational, dimension of hope.

Hope is something that breaks the framework of causality. When the effect far surpasses what is apparently the cause, and reverses the logical order, we are in the realm of hope and its mystery. Moreover, human history itself amply bears witness how the most unpredictable bursts into the theatre of human life, falsifying all ready-made scripts. Concurring with this seem to be the conclusions of physical sciences postulating a principle of indeterminacy as part and parcel of even material reality.[6]

Religions have interpreted this experience from a transcendental point of view. Hope became the never-receding horizon in their lives. Individual stories like those of Joseph (Gen. 37.12ff.) and Daniel (Dan. 6.1–29), and visions like that of Ezekiel (Ezek. 37.1–14) of the dry bones nurtured unshakeable confidence in a future which God had in store for his people. In the words of Walter Brueggemann, 'Old Testament is fundamentally a literature of hope'.[7]

The mystery and transcendence in the experience of hope can be seen in many other Asian traditions. Running through the Asian religious universe is the theme of the powerless conquering the mighty, the good ultimately triumphing over the powers of evil. Among many Asian peoples, popular celebration connected with myths inspired by this vision are occasions for a general renewal of hope. These stories and myths also have great significance as strategies for survival in the midst of odds. Particularly important are the myths of avatars of Vishnu in Hinduism. Avatars are stories of divine intervention to support the human family and the whole creation on its path to ultimate fullness and wholeness, and these occur, as the Bhagavad Gita notes, whenever *dharma* (righteousness) declines and *adharma* (unrighteousness) reigns over the world.[8] According to Hindu belief, the present age is a *kaliyuga* – an age of great calamity, misery, pain and hopelessness. A transformation in the present order of things is expected through the arrival of the final divine avatar, which is known as *kalkin*. The ultimate hope towards which one needs to move is the *lokasamgraha* or the well-being of all and of the entire cosmos.

Three Asian dreams

It is difficult to portray the wide expanse of the dreams of Asian peoples. These dreams differ depending on one's social location, class, caste, etc. Elementary psychology would tell us that the dreams reveal the person. The rich and powerful may have fabulous dreams towards the fulfilment of which they strive and compete. But if we take the poor of Asia, their dreams may amaze us by its very elementary character. In South Asia, where about 60% of the children are undernourished, what could be the dream of a child other than to have a full plate of rice? The dreams of the poor of Asia touch upon the most basic things in life.

It seems to me that beneath the dreams of the marginalized of Asia there lie three deep yearnings: to redeem power from its iniquity; to expand the sphere of freedom; and to be accepted in one's difference, which is a matter of identity, dignity and justice. Christianity becomes a historical agent of transforming hope to the extent it responds to these three dreams, as Jesus responded to the dream of the marginalized Palestinians of his times.[9]

Redeeming power: the service of hope

We do not require a Michel Foucault to tell us that power is entrenched in every realm of life, including our discourses.[10] It is a matter of everyday experience in Asia. If there is a general world-trend from coercion (raw power) in the direction of consent (however, not always free consent but often also engineered and manufactured consent!), we in Asia also have the reverse process, namely a movement from consent to coercion. The masses of the people, on the other hand, yearn to be freed from the daily stranglehold of iniquitous powers and want themselves to be the architects of their own destiny by participation in what concerns their life and their future. And yet what they experience is powerlessness and progressive exclusion.

It is in this context of disenchantment with the ruling powers and a sense of helplessness that Christianity could significantly contribute to the empowerment of the people. Hope is awakened among people when they see the prospects of transforming power from being a domination over to become a power as enablement. Experience shows that wherever in Asia Christian involvement went in the direction of assisting people to challenge the abuse of power, it brought a flash of hope into the unending tunnel of darkness. On the other hand, whenever the church placed the security of its institutions above the hope of the people, it added to the prevailing darkness.

Today, against the overall situation of servitude generated by the exercise of power as dominion over, Christianity can hold out hope for the people by contributing to create a general culture of servanthood.[11] Understanding of power in terms of servanthood is not to be confined to the Christian communities alone. This realization needs to become the order of the day in the various realms of life where power is exercised.

We may name two forces in Asia at work which create servitude. First of all, the forces of globalization have made it that those who have power and money are the ones before whom people should bend their knees. Power and money are the modern universals that transcend geographic region, culture, language, religion and so on. A second source of servitude derives from the Asian tradition, and it is different in different regions of the continent. In South Asia, for example, the hierarchization in the ordering of society by way of the ascriptive identity of caste has been a source of servitude. Both these sources of slavery in 'holy alliance' drive people into desperation and without prospects.

The prayer of an Asian poet seems to lend voice to the aspirations of the people to which Christians can meaningfully respond through their service of hope.

> This is my prayer to thee, my lord – strike at the root of penury in my heart . . . Give me the strength never to disown the poor or bend my knees before insolent might.[12]

Expansion of freedom: guarding the future

Hope of the Asian people grows to the extent their freedom expands. Freedom here is not to be understood as freedom from or simple autonomy of the individual but as enablement which is a substantive freedom, to be distinguished from formal freedom.[13] Without literacy, food, shelter, primary health care and social security, there is no true freedom for the Asian masses. The process that leads to the fulfilment of these Asian dreams, is, in effect, a process of true freedom.

So too, the creation of social opportunities for the full flowering of individuals and groups is a matter of cultivating freedom. In this sense, any authentic and integral development has to be understood as a realization of freedom. This has been well articulated by Amartya Sen, the Nobel laureate in economics.[14] Poverty forces individuals and families and communities into the alienation of their rights: prostitution, child labour, slavery, sale of human organs and mutilation of the body to enhance the capacity to beg. A life of dignity is impossible in the midst of poverty.[15]

All over Asia there are peoples and groups very much active at the grassroots who hold out hope for the people courageously by their commitment to freedom and human rights. We may think of the young people who valiantly stood for the cause of human rights and resisted their infringement, in spite of the violent crackdown by the Chinese regime at T'ien-an-men Square in June 1989.[16] Christians and Christian communities have proved themselves to be a source of hope wherever they have involved themselves to the freedom and human rights of the marginalized.[17] A case in point is the participation of Christians and different Christian churches in Korea for the cause of democracy.

Lived pluralism: defence of the poor

Plurality has been the hallmark of Asian life, and without it Asia loses all hope for its future. What is common to all the regions of Asia is the penetration of globalization.[18] According to analysts, globalization has created a threefold model of cultural change: one is the 'clash of civilizations', the second is homogenization or the so-called 'McDonaldization' of the world, and the third is hybridization.[19]

All these processes are at work in Asia. However, the most dominant one is the process of homogenization. Besides this, there are many traditional forms of homogenization specific to various countries and regions of Asia. In India, for example, the religious nationalism called 'Hindutva' is an ideology of homogenization which has a programme of unity that disregards the fact of pluralism of cultures and traditions in the country.[20] It is interesting to note that this programme of uniformity is an agenda of upper castes and classes, and is attuned to the realization of their interests, whereas for the marginal people it is pluralism that is of great importance for their life and survival.

If that is so, it is obvious why a church that wants to be on the side of the poor in Asia has to promote pluralism and should not fall prey to any monolithic conception and practice of unity. In other words, it is by promoting the regional, the local, the 'different', that Christianity will be a sign of hope to the marginalized peoples of Asia.

This last point needs some elaboration. I think that pluralism in Asia is ultimately a question of justice. Denial of pluralism kills justice before destroying true unity. It is by affirming the 'difference' that the poor have a chance to reclaim their very selves. Pluralism is thus the defence as well as the hope of the poor against the powerful who stand for an agenda of pseudo-unity. In this scenario, the hope-giving role that the church could play is to be an active agent of pluralism. But if the church itself is gripped by the fear of pluralism, it is incapacitated from the start to act truly as a catalyst of hope for the Asian poor.

Hope-generating Christian praxis in Asia

We know that the fulfilment of historical and earthly hopes are not opposed to the integral Christian vision of the future. In fact, the Old Testament vibrates with the expectations of the people for their physical needs and well-being (cf. Lev. 26.3–13). Jesus himself was so very attentive to human suffering and ailments, material needs and daily bread. Even though a certain 'spiritualization' takes place in the New Testament, nevertheless it never amounted to the neglect of the material needs of human beings. The focus on the poor in Jesus' message of the kingdom of God, the inextricable unity between love of neighbour and love of God, the early Christian position regarding private possessions, and the realization in the Middle Ages that the poor are the vicars of Christ (Matt. 25.31–45)[21] – all these attest to the power of the Christian life and message to awaken hope among the Asian poor. Christianity gives life to them in as much as it gives hope by living out the implications of the gospel. It is interesting to note that the poor found hope in early Christianity, because it made theirs what was considered to be the privilege of the elites: freedom, knowledge, power, community, etc.

Authentic Christian life in Asia needs a praxis of hope that would move from accumulation to emptiness, from individualism to hope-conferring solidarity, from distrust to positive appreciation of the human, from conformism to imagining alternatives. In this way, the church will give concrete shape to God's hope for the world.

Conclusion

'The birth of every child reminds us that God is not yet tired of human beings', wrote the poet Rabindranath Tagore.[22] In the birth of that child which will mark the year 2000 we celebrate the hope of God for the world. It is an occasion for all humankind to rejoice, and hence any sectarian, triumphalistic or exclusivistic celebration will only go against the universalistic opening that this birth represents. Asian Christians will therefore celebrate the occasions with all those peoples of the continent who venerate Jesus in various ways, cherish his ideals and allow themselves to be inspired by his example. Without them and their joy, how could the celebration of the great jubilee be complete?

The impending jubilee is also an occasion for the Asian Christian communities to reflect on the hope they are offering to the Asian masses and the tasks that it involves. No one can forget that fifty-five per cent of humanity lives in Asia alone. At one level, the task before us can be identified as one of redeeming power, expanding freedom and promoting pluralism. These vibrate with the dreams of the Asian peoples for a different order of society that is just, humane, harmonious and compassionate. At another level, we realize the deeper and spiritual dimension when we come to understand that it is by the praxis of self-emptying that hope is awakened and that through solidarity it is sustained. For hope to flourish, it requires the Christian communities to exude a positive outlook on the human. Finally, it is the capacity of the Christian communities to imagine alternatives that will bring about a true encounter between the Asian dreams and the Christian hope as we step into the year 2000.

Notes

1. Cf. Gandhi, *What Jesus Means to Me*, Ahmedabad 1959; Swami Ranganthananda, *The Christ We Adore*, Calcutta [7]1996; Hans Staffner, *The Significance of Jesus Christ in Asia*, Anand 1985; M. M. Thomas, *The Acknowledged Christ of the Indian Renaissance*, London 1970.

2. Brian K. Smith, *Classifying the Universe. The Ancient Indian Varna System and the Origins of Caste*, New York and Oxford 1994, 172.

3. It may be recalled here that the chronology of a Christian era starting from the birth of Jesus was inroduced in the sixth century and owes its origin to the Scythian monk Dionysius Exiguus. Even in the West, there have been, obviously, many calendars with different points of reference. Christians followed the Julian calendar even while they evolved a specifically Christian one.

4. Dominique Lapierre, *A Thousand Suns*, Delhi 1999.

5. The lotus is a flower very much loved and cherished among the Asian peoples. The fact that it blooms from out of the muddy ground under the waters is the symbol of great, noble and beautiful things emerging from destitution, distress and affliction.

6. Cf. Jayant V. Narlikar, 'Quantum Uncertainty and the Response of the Universe', in *Philosophy of Science. Perspectives from Natural and Social Sciences*, Simla 1992, 69–72; Kamila Datta, 'Determinism and Chaos in Classical and Quantum Physics', ibid., 77–85; D. S. Chattopadhyaya, 'Chance and Determinism', ibid., 105–17.

7. Walter Brueggemann, *Hope within History*, Atlanta 1987, 72; id., *Hopeful Imagination. Prophetic Voices in Exile*, Philadelphia 1988; cf. also M. Maria Arul Raja, 'Assertion of the Periphery. Some Biblical Paradigms', *Jeevadhara*, 1997, 25–35.

8. Bhagavadgita IV, 7–8: Lord Krishna speaks to Arjuna: 'Whenever there is a

decline of righteousness and rise of unrighteousness . . . then I send forth (create, incarnate) Myself.' Cf. Geoffrey Parrinder, *Avatar and Incarnation. A Comparison of Indian and Christian Belief*, New York 1982.

9. This article does not intend to deal comprehensively with the theme of Christian eschatology. These are some very limited reflections bearing on the contemporary Asian context.

10. Hubert L. Dreyfus and Paul Rabinow, *Michel Foucault. Beyond Structuralism and Hermeneutics*, Chicago 1983; Peter Dews, *Logics of Disintegration. Post-Structuralist Thought and the Claims of Critical Theory*, London and New York 1987.

11. Felix Wilfred, 'Church's Commitment to the Poor in the Age of Globalization', in *Colloquium on Church in Asia in the 21st Century*, Manila 1998, 211–27.

12. Rabindranath Tagore, *Gitanjali*, New Delhi and New York 1918, no. 36.

13. A similar differentiation in terms of material and formal is made by Enrique Dussel in the field of ethics in his dialogue with discourse ethics and transcendental pragmatics (J. Habermas, K. Otto-Apel), cf. *Etica de la liberacion en la edad de la globalizacion y de la exclusion*, Madrid 1998.

14. Cf. Amartya Sen, *On Ethics and Economics*, Delhi 1987; Sen distinguishes five kinds of freedom: internal, participatory, transactional, procedural and protective. Cf. *Frontline*, 6 November 1998, 10 and 11. Cf. also Amartya Sen and James D. Wolfensohn, 'Development: A Coin with Two Sides', *The Hindu*, 6 May 1999, 11.

15. Asian Human Rights Commission (AHRC), *Our Common Humanity: The Asian Charter on Human Rights*, Hong Kong, no. 2.4.

16. Cf. Immanuel C. Y. Hsu, *The Rise of Modern China*, Oxford and New York [7]1995, 927ff.

17. *Human Rights and the Church in Asia: Thematic Report of the 1st Asian Human Rights Workshop, Bangkok, August 2–9, 1997*, Fribourg 1997; cf. also *For All the Peoples of Asia. Federation of Asian Bishops' Conferences Documents from 1970–1996*, Vols I and II, Manila 1987, 1997.

18. On globalization from an Asia–Pacific perspective, cf. the contribution of the Malaysian thinker, Chandra Muzzafar, 'Globalization. The Perceptions, Experiences and Responses of the Religious Traditions and Cultural Communities in the Asia Pacific Region', in *Colloquium on Church in Asia in the 21st Century* (n. 11), 33–43. For an overall analysis, cf. Daniel Cohen, *Richesse du monde, pauvreté des nations*, Paris 1997; Hans-Peter Martin and Harald Schumann, *Die Globalisierungsfalle. Der Angriff auf Democratie und Wohlstand*, Frankfurt [16]1997.

19. Cf. Jan Nederveen Pieterse, 'Globalization and Culture: Three Paradigms', *Economic and Political Weekly*, XXXI, 22 January 1996, 1389–93.

20. Cf. Christophe Jaffrelot, *Les nationalistes hindoues*, Paris 1993.

21. Cf. Michel Mollat, *Les Pauvres au Moyen Age*, Paris 1978.

22. Rabindranath Tagore, *Stray Birds*, New York 1916, no. 77.

A Jubilee in Jeans

Donna Singles

An old man submerged in a sea of frenzied young admirers: the spectacle of a Pope surrounded by youth from practically every country in the world leaves few people indifferent. It's an important lesson, especially for the melancholy prophets of doom who are unhappy over the desertion of their parishes by the young.

Indeed, the attraction that youth feel for the Pope is so universal that even countries whose religious practice is in free-fall will be represented at the jubilee. Organizers of the last 'World Youth Days' are still smarting from the memory of their embarrassment when so many other youth besides those close to church circles answered the Pope's call. They were hardly prepared for the mass of teenagers – and less than teen – that descended on them during the events of 1997.

Youth from the West

The great diversity of young people who will participate in Jubilee 2000 makes it impossible to generalize. The decision to consider in this article only the youth of 'developed' or Western countries is based simply on the author's own experience. Attention will be focussed particularly on the young who are not yet fully integrated into the adult world by reason of work or conjugal responsibilities: high schoolers, college students, apprentices, youth in military service . . . They are to be found in the chaplaincies of schools or universities, in scout movements, base communities and centres of spiritual formation.

The list also includes young people open to religious ideas who keep a decided distance from any church. These are youth who pursue their spiritual journey with no thought of permanent engagement, which explains their willingness to participate in short-term activities such as pilgrimages, days of reflexion, youth retreats or brief stays in a monastery.

With these particular youth in mind, we ask: What do they expect from Jubilee 2000? What meaning may the event have for them? Both questions merit consideration here.

What youth expects from Jubilee 2000

Young people, especially those concerned about the rights of human beings or ecology, might well discover something in common with the spirit of hope underlying the Judaeo–Christian concept of jubilee. They could find an incentive, for example, in the radical demands that Yahweh made on his people during the jubilee year: forgiveness of debts, liberation of slaves, forbidding exploitation of others and letting the land lie fallow (cf. Lev. 25.8–54). Understood as precursors of the new order that God intended for his people, such imperatives could be seen by youth as a call to their own generosity. God also invites them to work for greater solidarity in a world more respectful of its inhabitants and its resources. Indeed, the biblical theme of jubilee is eminently appropriate for awakening in youth a desire to work for these goals.

The need for such an awakening has never been greater. Admittedly, many young people are idealists, donating their time and energy to generous causes. At the same time, adults similarly engaged in such efforts are disarmed by the absence in youth of ideological motives for their involvement.

A second reason makes such an awakening necessary: the growing attraction to youth of paranormal phenomena. The search for peak experience leads those who are most easily influenced or alienated from the world of adults to put their confidence in esoteric practices which they feel to be more in accordance with their expectations.

Were they asked why they refuse to place their spiritual search under the guidance of traditional religious leaders, the response could well take the form of a certain impatience with unverifiable religious beliefs or moral codes frozen in history. For example, one young person declares, 'I need to feel close to the invisible, but not by going to church. When I see an object move by itself or a sick person suddenly cured, that says more to me than a mass where nothing happens.'

Another will admit that he prefers yoga exercises or transcendental meditation which do not require him to believe in dogmas he does not understand. The conclusion is clear: today, spiritual relativism, 'New Age' or other occult practices are more acceptable to youth than ecclesiastical absolutism.

Sadly enough, authority figures in whom they can trust seem to be in short supply. Surprisingly, perhaps, one adult retains their confidence:

the Pope. 'He tells us what the law is', says one relieved teenager, in spite of the fact that he knows almost nothing of the Bible, the sacraments or life in his local parish.

This leaves us with the paradox of young people who on the one hand do not expect the Pope to preach to them about morality and on the other want the 'representative of God on earth' to be a father figure for them, reassuring them by saying 'Be not afraid!' Indeed, John Paul II is well-known for his desire to see jubilee become a factor of renewed hope in the young, including non-Catholics.

However, youths from Protestant churches in France were deeply disappointed when the Catholic organizers of the 1997 'World Youth Days' refused their request to meet with the Pope and have him sign their 'Charter on Living Together'. The answer they received dashed all hope of any such meeting taking place: 'This is not the way ecumenism is done in the Catholic Church', said one indignant bishop responsible for the events. As for the president of the Conference of French Bishops, he simply compounded the issue by giving the non-Catholic youth to understand that they should not count on the bishops to encourage their initiative.

Burned by the experience, young Protestants might well hesitate to accept the Pope's invitation to take part in the next jubilee. In any case, they have no reason to think that their charter will find a place on the agenda of Jubilee 2000. Whether or not they decide to join their Catholic friends for the event, they already know they would do well to lower their expectations.

Jubilee 2000 raises a second and related question: what meaning might young people in the West draw from the event? One wonders about the significance of a church-related celebration for young people whose knowledge of their religious and spiritual traditions is decidedly wanting.

The meaning of jubilee for youth

Living in a society where almost no boundaries exist that state what boys and girls may or may not do, and where 'mixity' dominates social codes, such young people are particularly at ease in the quasi-'unisex' world created by Youth Days. The social cohesion generated by the situation could easily lead them to suppose that, at least temporarily, all divisions have been healed (with one exception: the separation between young and old). Such a sexually liberated generation might well see jubilee as prophetic, as a sign of humanity purified of all conflict and discrimination, even between the sexes.

Girls in particular will be attentive to this obviously utopian aspect of jubilee. Hence they could be forgiven for wondering why a celebrating church that proclaims the end of all inequalities refuses, at the same time, the idea of eliminating remaining barriers to women's advancement in society. Worse still, the church itself offers no real choices to women in its own ecclesiastical life.

Obviously, jubilee is not created for in-depth questioning. A crowd's capacity to dissolve distances in a temporary but powerful conglomerate of many individuals readily becomes a short-circuit for numbing one's normal judgment. Only later, with return to daily reality, will the hard questions surface again. The natural tolerance of youth caught up in the overheated atmosphere of mass euphoria is easily transformed into an attitude of indifference towards all differences. However, such simplifications are not likely to disturb the young. This kind of minimization is already reflected in their present 'credo': freedom of choice for all and the liberty of each to live as he chooses. In a word, hard-line positions are out.

While this is not the message the church wants to convey to the young, it is the one getting through to them, for example in the area of ecumenism. By extending a welcome to 'all men of good will', the jubilee celebration may even boomerang. Whether or not the church intends it, the new attitude of openness towards its 'sister churches' may be understood by the young as a sign that Rome has renounced its past claim to superiority. In the light of the apparent disappearance of Rome's absolute stance of the past, the young might even interpret this to mean acceptance of other churches as equals. Indeed, there is no question that they would by happy to see dialogue renewed not only between Christians, but also between Jews and Moslems.

So expectations are running high. The bottom line still remains, however: the difficulty of consolidating results of jubilee. How will values manifested in the enthusiasm of a mass gathering be solidly rooted? Certainly, the young will be heartened – at least for a time – by the heady experience of seeing so many young Christians share the same faith. They will also be happy to take part in the small workshops that are a familiar part of Youth Days.

In the end, however, possibilities for serious thought will remain largely problematic. The big question will be how to invent durable forms of involvement in keeping with their understanding of faith and expectations rather than those of the institutional church. A difficult task indeed! Parents, in particular, worry that their children's sub-culture is too much at odds with their own way of living as Christians.

And since ultimate decisions regarding Jubilee 2000 always lie with the highest authorities in the church – elderly, celibate men having little or no contact with the young – it is difficult to avoid asking: Will such men really be able to understand the discouragement of parents in the face of their children's indifference towards organized religion? It is unlikely.

Certainly, the young approve the church's idea to offer them a fabulous occasion like jubilee to come together. But they are not duped. They are perfectly aware that an event as fleeting as Jubilee 2000 will not answer their deepest spiritual needs. With no follow-up to help them to interpret the meaning and finality of jubilee, there is real risk of a bitter after-taste, especially for the young who have no solid faith community to go back to. Youth Days are too grandiose, too disconnected from daily life.

For example, youth are well aware of the Pope's frequent call to conversion. But what does conversion mean to young people at the beginning of their lives? In the final analysis, they have little sympathy with platitudes that are unrelated to the real world in which they live: a society built on consumerism, profit and trivialized sex.

Who will tell them, for example, that true conversion is not simply a private affair of confessing one's sins or of obtaining indulgences? Who will tell them that true conversion means stripping oneself naked, so to speak, in order to put priorities where they belong: helping men and women to live together in hope in spite of a world that seems bent on self-destruction? This is surely a message that young people are capable of receiving and of putting into practice.

Hopefully, the values of jubilee will not be drowned out by the chorus of unrepressed and somewhat mindless cries of adulation for a single individual. No one denies the Pope's gift for capturing the hearts and minds of young people. But by the same token, few people would agree that he has equally succeeded in persuading youth to engage in the church's work.

In the end, we can hope simply that Jubilee 2000 will bring youth closer to the gospel and to the values enshrined in the event: universality and unity of the human family. Were that to happen, the first Youth Days of the twenty-first century will already have scored a touch-down!

III · Hope and Grace

Resurrection: The Ground, Power and Goal of our Hope

Jürgen Moltmann

I. The historical situation: beginning of the future – end of the world?

Any hermeneutic of Christian hope is governed by the political context, the historical *kairos* and the human community in which we ask about the future and about hope. The historical situation at the turn of the millennium is directly governed by the age of progress and the age of annihilation. The nineteenth century saw the construction of the Western world, which today has turned into the modern world. The twentieth century experienced the self-destruction of the Christian world from which these two worlds emerged, in the two European World Wars.[1]

The nineteenth century was a century of beginnings, of promises and of utopias. The industrial revolution promised prosperity for all and the greatest happiness for the greatest possible number of people. The democratic revolution in the USA and France promised 'freedom – equality – brotherhood': 'sisterhood' had to be added later. The socialist revolution was to complete the democratic revolution by the 'classless society' in the 'realm of freedom'. It was to begin an era of 'eternal peace' (as Kant remarked). Belief in progress, spurred on by ever new scientific discoveries and technical inventions, trusted in a beginning without end and a future of unlimited possibilities. Theologically speaking, it was chiliasm turned secular. What earlier generations had only hoped for and had lacked was now to be capable of 'realization': the kingdom of God, the kingdom of freedom, the golden age. The Christian great powers shared out the rest of the world in their colonial empires, certainly with the evil intent of dominating and exploiting the world, but also with the good intent of educating and developing humankind. The churches welcomed the nineteenth century as the 'Christian Century' and the modern world as the 'Christian World', to mention the titles of an American and a German journal. The optimism of global progress also stamped the great philosophical systems of the consummation of the world, which governed the thinking of the dominant peoples. Everyone spoke of 'world history', though by this they meant only their own world.

By contrast the twentieth century became the 'age of anxiety'. It became the century of the end, the century of destruction. In the First World War the Christian great powers of Europe destroyed each other. In the Second World War the Germans started on the annihilation. It was the end of Europe. 'Weapons of mass destruction' were manufactured and used: in the First World War poison gas, in the Second World War atom bombs. The nihilistic Nazi dictatorship wanted the 'final solution' of the Jewish question and set up the mass extermination camps which under the name 'Auschwitz' brought eternal shame upon us. The nihilistic Stalinists annihilated unwanted masses by work and sickness in the 'Gulag Archipelago'. A nihilistic delight in mass murders seized China, Cambodia, Rwanda, Serbia and other countries. No century has seen such crimes against humanity as the twentieth century, which could and would still realize the hopes, promises and utopias of the nineteenth century. No one today can guarantee an end to these destructions. 'Scientific civilization' is spreading its lines of communication all over the earth like a spider's web, and with the human seizure of power over nature has also brought in the 'end of nature'. People living in the dominant world are no longer stamped by the hybris of belief in progress but by the melancholy of the disappointments and destructions that they have suffered. The active hope which changes the world seems to have emigrated to the poor people of the Third World.

With the end of the deadly threat which the world posed to itself in the 'Cold War' waged by the superpowers, in which life stagnated, in 1989 people began to experience a certain return of the beginnings of the nineteenth century in the 'globalization' of markets and the media of the Western world so that they became 'one world'. Whatever does not fit into this fine new world is said not to be part of it, and those who are not among the global players are rapidly made 'surplus people' and suppressed. In this global situation after the 'century of beginnings', and after the 'century of the end', is there rebirth of hope which holds for all life, all human beings and all the earth, and is not coupled with the threat of annihilation of other people and other things?

II. The resurrection of the crucified, dead Christ

Christian hope is not the religious interpretation of the positive and negative trends of human history but stems from the *memoria Christi*.[2] Certainly human optimism about the future is surpassed in Christian history and in the Christian present by the chiliastic vision of the possibility of bringing history to its consummation, and human anxieties about the future take on a deeper religious dimension through the apocalyptic horrors which depict the catastrophic breaking off of human history. No one is really free from this: if things go better, we think that the kingdom of God is near; if they go worse, we think that God's judgment is coming upon us. But these religious interpretations of human hopes and anxieties are not Christian. Christian hope is grounded in the memory and the making present of Christ. It is the hope of Christ; otherwise it is not 'Christian'. It is remembered hope, because it seeks the future of Christ in the past of Christ and finds it in the resurrection of the crucified and dead Christ. Therefore Christian hope is always bound up with the remembrance of the suffering of Christ and his death on the cross. 'The resurrection of the crucified Christ' says that a new beginning is to be found in his end on the cross, and with him for the world. 'The resurrection of the dead Christ' says that he is not among the dead and thus the order of this mortal world is broken through. By his death on the cross Christ is taken away from the living; by his resurrection he is taken away from the dead. The male disciples fled with great terror from the helpless dying of their Messiah on Golgotha; the female disciples who endured the horror of his crucifixion fled from his tomb in shock at his resurrection from the dead. By virtue of the resurrection of Christ, Christian hope arises from this twofold 'zero point': the disciples' crucified future hope of the disciples and the women's destroyed trust in death.

(a) *The crucified future hope*. The flight of the disciples from the scene of Christ's crucifixion and the denial of Peter are well attested in the Gospels. The Gethsemane story is the key story. Christ's prayer is not heard by God, whom here he calls 'Abba, dear Father' (Mark 14.36); Judas 'betrays' him to the Romans (14.44); Peter, from whom the first confession of Christ comes (8.29), denies him three times (14.66-72); 'and the disciples all forsook him and fled' (14.50). 'Abandoned' by God and human beings, Jesus dies a solitary death on a Roman cross. 'Betrayed', 'denied', 'forsaken': these are not just references to human weaknesses and faithlessness but reactions to terrible disappointments. 'Blessed is the kingdom of our father David that is coming' is the jubilant greeting with which the people welcome Jesus on his entry into Jerusalem (Mark 11.10). 'But we had hoped that he would redeem Israel', lament the fleeing disciples in Emmaus (Luke 24.21). For those who had forsaken all and followed him, this messianic hope for the restoration of the kingdom of David and liberation from the Roman occupying forces is cruelly disappointed by the unexpected weakness of Jesus. Therefore their love turns to hatred. They betrayed, denied and abandoned the one by whom they felt betrayed, denied and abandoned. Jesus' crucifixion is the end of their hope.

(b) *The destroyed trust in death.* The male disciples abandoned Jesus in terror at the crucifixion which he so impotently endured, but the women remained loyal to the dying man 'and looked on from afar'. They are also mentioned by name (Mark 15.40). Evidently death was no stranger to them, and Jesus' death was not the end of their love. Mary Magdalene, Mary mother of James, and Salome went to the tomb of their friend and master when the sabbath was past. They found the tomb empty and heard the voice of an angel: 'He has risen, he is not here' (Mark 16.6). Only at this moment were they seized with 'trembling and astonishment' (16.8) and were afraid. This is no Easter joy in jubilation at the resurrection, but cold dismay. Like birth, so too death belongs to the finitude of human existence. Therefore trust in natural life includes trust in natural death. What seized the women with the uttermost dismay at the empty tomb of Jesus was the collapse of this world order of life and death. The basis for the order of this mortal life shook under their feet. Even death is no longer certain, and we are no longer certain about the dead, for the dead no longer find rest before the creative God. In its origin the mystery of the resurrection, which was later felt to be so miraculous, was and remains by nature a dismaying *mysterium tremendum.*

(c) *The new reality of the resurrection.* Any analysis of the Easter accounts of the disciples in Galilee and the women in Jerusalem shows the uniquely new reality in which the dead Christ evidently appeared to them. This was no reanimation or return of the dead man. They did not recognize him in his new reality. He 'showed himself' or was 'revealed' to them. First of all he had to be identified by the marks of his wounds from the cross, in his breaking of the bread and with his voice. When the disciples on the Emmaus Road recognized him, 'he immediately vanished from their sight' (Luke 24.31). He revealed himself to them 'in another form' (Mark 16.12). His 'appearances' evoked 'unbelief', not 'faith', as Mark 16(.11, 14, 13) reports. 'Doubts' overcame the disciples, as the story of Thomas relates (John 20.24–29). It is the Christ who appears who first calls on them to 'believe'

(Mark 16.14; John 20.27). The Easter stories thus describe that new, incomparable reality for Christ, for which those concerned used the eschatological category of the 'resurrection of the dead' and the 'life of the world to come'. No one saw what happened to the crucified, dead Christ. But he 'appeared' bodily in the transfigured form (Phil. 3.21) of the world of the resurrection that changes everything. Therefore his resurrection cannot be added to his death as a further 'historical event', linked with a narrative 'and'. It belongs in another category. As an eschatological event his resurrection relates not only to his life after death but to the whole story of his life from the manger to the cross. On the basis of his resurrection from the dead the whole Christ is present in the Spirit which brings life.

(d) *The collective resurrection of Christ.* In the modern world we have become accustomed to understanding persons as individuals. But as the Synoptic Gospels tell it, the history of Christ is always also the history of his people, whether this is the people of Israel, with whose recollections the story of Christ is told, or the history of the homeless people (*ochlos*), with whose suffering his history is depicted. Therefore the resurrection of Christ, too, is no individual resurrection. He is raised as the Christ of Israel, the head of the church and the pioneer of a new humanity, as the 'new Adam' and not least as the 'firstborn of all creation' (Col. 1.15). The Eastern icons of the Orthodox Church show that pictorially: the resurrection of Christ begins in the world of the dead. The risen Christ draws Adam with his right hand and Eve with his left, and with them the whole of humankind and the whole 'sighing creation' from the world of death to the transfigured world of the eternal life of the new creation. Christ's death on the cross was exclusive and lonely, but his resurrection is inclusive, open to the world and embracing the universe: a cosmic event, the beginning of the new creation of all things.

(e) *The overcoming of sin, death and hell.* With the overcoming of the crucified hope of the disciples and the destroyed trust in death of the women, the primitive Christian faith in the resurrection acted in the ancient world like an explosion of hearts and senses. With elemental force it attacked the 'powers of this world': the violence of sin, the inevitability of death and the hopelessness of hell. The risen Christ became the power of protest against these godless powers that were hostile to humankind. If the one who was crucified by the power of the Roman state has been raised by God who has created heaven and earth, then God can be trusted in deep godforsakenness and hope where no more can be hoped for. For 'he will destroy every rule and every authority and every power' (I Cor. 15.24). Therefore the murderers will not finally triumph over their victims. If the Crucified One has been given his right by God, then there is justice for all who suffer violence. The one who guarantees this justice is present himself in the risen Christ. If Christ is risen 'from the dead', then the end of death is in sight: 'The last enemy to be destroyed is death' (I Cor. 15.26). That is the beginning of the immortality of all that is mortal, 'and death will be no more' (Rev. 21.4). 'Death is swallowed up in the victory of life', says the primitive Christian Easter hymn (I Cor. 15.55). The destroyed trust in death turns into the jubilation of eternal life. As the later Christian martyrs show, this jubilation overcomes the fear of death with which all violent rulers oppress the people. Not least, Christian belief saw in the resurrection of the godforsaken Christ the destruction of 'hell': 'Hell, where is your victory?' (I Cor. 15.55). 'Hell' means situations of deep godforsakenness and total hopelessness, situations of torment without prospect of an end. The resurrection of the godforsaken Christ overcomes not only temporal death but also 'eternal death', the death of God. All the Easter hymns sing of the 'destruction of hell' by the resurrection of the crucified Christ. Since Christ's 'descent into hell' there is hope where all prospects vanish: 'Even in hell you are there' (Ps. 139.8).[3]

III. Living in the power of the resurrection today

In the twenty-first century we shall take up the unfulfilled promises and hopes of the nineteenth century once more, since there is no alternative to the market economy, constitutional democracy, sustained ecology and a culture of life. But with these visions we will have to live over those abysses of crimes against humanity, mass annihilations and destructions of the earth which we have experienced in the twentieth century. The coming centuries also belong to the 'end time', in that exterminism is possible at any time and everywhere. If we can again draw hope for a better future, it will be a future with mourning over our lost innocence and anxiety about the countless possibilities of annihilation. If humankind is to survive, we need an affirmation of life which is stronger than anxiety about the possibilities of mass annihilation and a transcendent 'courage to be', despite the very real possibilities of 'nothingness'.[4] I find such an affirmation of life and such courage to be in the power of the resurrection, which lives from the remembrance of the crucified Christ and awaits the annihilation of death and the 'life of the world to come'. The power of the resurrection shows itself in the 'anticipations of God's kingdom, showing now something of the newness which Christ will complete',[5] and in the consolations which support us through suffering, so that we are preserved and do not have to give up. This can be demonstrated in three dimensions:

(a) *Life against death.* Death is not only the natural end of a finite life but a destructive power which towers up into personal, social and creaturely life.[6] The powers of death are oppression, exploitation, sickness and alienation. We have before our eyes the pictures of the starving children of the Third World and the exposed street children in the slums of the big cities; we know the number of those suffering from AIDS in Black Africa; we know about the raped women and murdered men in Bosnia and the massacres in Algeria; we have 'superfluous' life, without work and without meaning, before our own doors. Death is in no way just a fate but a power hostile to life, against which one must live and fight, for too many healthy and strong people have made a covenant with the death of others and live at the cost of poorer and weaker people. Life against these powers of death means loving, sharing life, establishing life and making life once again worth living. 'Love is as strong as death,' we read in the Song of Songs, for it is 'a flame of the Lord'. 'We have passed from death to life because we love . . .', the first Christians said of themselves (I John 3.14). In love of common life we experience not only the natural forces of life but also already the 'powers of the world to come' (Heb. 6.5), i.e. those powers of the resurrection which one day will overcome death altogether. Living against death is therefore the meaning of any loved and loving life. The other side of this power lies in the consolation of the Spirit, which can establish and support us where our possibilities are at an end and we can do no more.

(b) *Justice against violence.* In view of what military, economic and ideological violence has done in the twentieth century, in the next centuries there will be no meaningful 'violent solutions' to the problems of humankind. Conflicts and problems which serve life can only be resolved in a non-violent way.[7] Any use of violence, even if it is meant to prevent violent actions, can escalate, get out of control and spark off the use of 'weapons of mass destruction'. However, peace in which life can develop is not yet the absence of violence, but the presence of justice. The alternative to the vicious circle of violence and counter-violence is the extension of justice. But what today are the criteria for a justice which serves the common life in peace? Today they are to be found all over the world and with growing assent in the Universal Declaration of Human Rights (1948) and the international pacts for social, economic and cultural rights (1966). Crimes against humanity are measured against this standard of human rights and are now condemned and punished in Europe in the Hague; in the future they will also be punished globally in international courts of justice. The United Nations will slowly but surely develop from an alliance of nations into an international community which imposes law. As non-governmental organizations, the Christian churches will strengthen the universal character of human rights over against national self-interest, since for them it is not a nation, but each human individual, who is in the 'image of God'. Their special contribution lies in transposing the divine justice they experience in faith into the practice of justice. The God who 'secures the rights of those who suffer violence' and who 'justifies' the unjust sinners makes possible both a creative justice, with which we take the side of those without rights, the poor and the weak, and a transforming justice, with which we confront the powerful, the rich and the strong. The God who creates and establishes justice is not only the embodiment of our experience of God but also our consolation: God's justice will triumph; the murderers will not finally triumph over their victims, for God is God.

(c) *Creation against annihilation*. The paradigm which governs science, technology, the economy and the media is the domination and exploitation of all things on this earth by human beings. This earth is regarded as a single sphere, the treasures and energies of which will be made 'resources' for the human world. Ever larger and ever fewer 'global players' divide out this sphere among themselves. Under their rule, closely-woven networks of movements in finance and trade come into being. In the sphere of the media the American cultural industry has triumphed. The rising world civilization is becoming ever more uniform. This globalization of human domination is ambivalent through and through: if everything is under our control and manipulable, then the potential for human beings to destroy the world also grows. In order to avoid the destructions of the earth it is good to take a stand for 'the preservation of creation' and to protect life through bioethical conventions. But this conservative ethic always comes too late. It is better to develop a counter-model of the continuation of creation. With the paradigm of 'indwelling' we say that humanity must find a place which furthers life in the household of the living on this 'blue planet'. It will find it by living together with other creatures, not exploiting and killing them. However, the scientific and technical potential of humankind which is to be developed further must not become a domination that destroys the world; it can also be used for a sustained agreement of human culture in the nature of this organism that is our earth. The creation 'earth' will then not only be preserved but also developed further towards its goal. For it is made the 'common home' of all earthly creatures and one day in the consummation is also to become the 'house of God' (Rev. 21.3). If God's indwelling is itself the goal of creation, then the destructions of the environments and the annihilations of living beings which we lament will not drive us to resignation and cynicism, but teach us the patience of hope and encourage us to persistent action for life.

God's great goal with the creation of all things from nothing and the resurrection of the crucified Christ from death is the indwelling of his glory, which transforms everything and brings it to life in the new, eternal creation (Rev. 21.1.5).[8]

Translated by John Bowden

Notes

1. *Is the World Ending? Concilium* 1998/4, ed. Sean Freyne and Nicholas Lash.
2. J. Moltmann, *The Way of Jesus Christ. Christology in Messianic Dimensions*, London 1990, Chapter V, The Eschatological Resurrection of Christ, 213–73; M. Welker, *Gottes Geist. Theologie des Heiligen Geistes*, Neukirchen 1992, Part 2: Der verheissene Geist der Gerechtigkeit und des Friedens, 109–73.
3. I think that the replacement of hell 'fire' by 'total non-being' as in the Doctrine Commission of the Church of England, *The Mystery of Salvation. The Story of God's Gift*, London 1996, 199, is theologically wrong. The issue is the overcoming of 'hell' by Christ's descent into hell, not its modernization.
4. Paul Tillich, *The Courage to Be*, London and New York 1952.
5. *Uppsala Speaks, Message of the Fourth Assembly of the World Council of Churches*, Geneva 1968, 1.
6. N. O. Brown, *Life against Death. The Psychoanalytical Meaning of History*, New York 1959.
7. J. Moltmann, *Creating a Just Future. The Politics of Peace and the Ethics of Creation in a Threatened World*, London and Philadelphia 1989.
8. J. Moltmann, *The Coming of God. Christian Eschatology*, London and Minneapolis 1996.

Sources of Hope

1. The Women's Movement
María Pilar Aquino

At the end of the second millennium, the women's movement is proving responsible for a major, epoch-making shift in the history of humankind. As a world-wide historical event and a force bearing a vision of fullness for the whole of creation, this movement is shaping a new paradigm of a civilization capable of upholding the intrinsic dignity of persons, the integral development of peoples, justice in human relations, and respect for eco-systems.

Rather than a body with well-defined contours, the women's movement is a dynamic historical process, building agendas from the interests and needs of women, working out contents rooted in the accumulated wisdom of women, making present the memory of our creations and resistances in history, putting forward platforms for action corresponding to changing historical circumstances, forming alliances among groups of women to confront widespread poverty and injustice, and nourishing the feminist vision of a humanity and an earth finally reconciled. As such, the women's movement is seen as a process that makes plaits, networks, webs, circles, fabrics and mosaics to bind together the actual dynamics of women's lives in both urban and rural environments. With varying forces, maturity, resources, opportunities and challenges, this movement is present in practically all the nations, religions and cultures in the world. Although its impact too varies, there is no doubt that it is producing a substantive change in value-systems and criteria for judgment, traditions of thought, social and political customs, cultural environments, the general feeling of nations, and people's ethical-religious understanding. This is why I call it a major, epoch-making shift in the history of humankind.

In the context of Christianity, the women's movement continues to apply pressure in both academic and pastoral fields with the aim of making the churches develop the necessary resources and apply the appropriate measures to change situations of injustice against women, in society in general as well as within the churches. It is true that the liberating traditions of Christianity have inspired the activities of many women in their quest for greater justice and human dignity. Nevertheless, it is also true that in their two thousand years of existence the institutions and official theology of the Christian churches have not yet made a serious and effective commitment to confronting injustices against women arising from racism, homophobia, violence and exclusion in all the forms these take.[1]

The women's movement is undoubtedly a major source of hope because it bears a message of liberation for the world and because its mission and aim are compatible with the liberating vision of the gospel. As a dynamic process in the renewal of history and humankind, this movement gives out a clear sign of the Spirit of God leading the world to new realities, toward its ultimate perfecting. I should like to back up my understanding of the women's movement as a source of hope with two recommendations and two observations. First, in order to see the magnitude, complexity and depth of this movement, visit a site on the Internet that provides ample information; I know it is not the only one, but this one does provide links that are of interest internationally: Women in Network.[2] Second, to understand the movement's depth of analysis and critical framework, read the final documents produced during the most recent International Women's Solidarity Meeting, which took place in Havana on 13–14 April 1998.[3] Third, the brief description I give here of the women's movement is based on my knowledge of the movement in the context of the Americas and focuses on civil organizations. Fourth, I recognize that the description is limited for reasons of space, but I still attempt to bring out its central characteristics.

1. *Profile*. As a socio-cultural force for change, the feminist and women's movement takes on various organizational forms (institutional and non-institutional, but generally non-governmental organizations); it takes shape as an autonomous space formed by women (but accepting mixed groups); it is embodied in: (*a*) meetings, such as 'Latin American and Caribbean Feminist Meetings'; (*b*) days, such as 'Central American Feminist Days'; (*c*) networks, such as 'Latin American and Caribbean Feminist Network against Domestic and Sexual Violence'; 'Network of Afro-Caribbean and Afro-Latin American Women' and 'Network for Popular Education among Women'; (*d*) units and programmes within broader institutions, such as the 'Women and Development Unit of the

Economic Commission for Latin America and the Caribbean' and 'Woman's Programme of the Dominican Centre for Education Studies'; (*e*) committees and fronts, such as the 'Latin American and Caribbean Committee for the Defence of Woman's Rights' and the 'Continental Front of Women for a Worthy Life'; (*f*) feminist centres and women's centres, such as the '"Flora Tristán" Peruvian Women's Centre' in Peru; the 'Feminist Centre for Information and Action' in Costa Rica; the 'Centre for Women's Projects' in Brazil; the '"Maria Quilla" Centre for Investigation and Education in the Condition of Women' in Ecuador; the 'Women's Centre for Communication, Exchange and Human Development in Latin America' in Mexico; the '"Gregoria Apaza" Centre for the Advancement of Women' in Bolivia and the 'Centre for Women's Rights' in Honduras; (*g*) study centres, such as the 'Nucleus for Studies in Violence' at the university of São Paulo in Brazil; (*h*) collectives and coalitions, such as the 'Radial Feminist Collective' in Peru and the 'Coalition against Traffic in Women' in Venezuela; (*i*) coordinators and councils, such as the 'Peace Coordinator for Women' in Puerto Rico and the 'Council of Mayan Women' in Guatemala; (*j*) feminist publishers and publications, such as ISIS: Women's International Editions, and FEMPRESS: Women's Alternative Communication Network in Chile; *La Boletina* from 'Meeting Points' in Nicaragua; 'Popular Feminist Editions' in the Dominican Republic; and *Cotidiano Mujur: Revista Feminista* (Woman's Daily: Feminist Review) in Uruguay; (*k*) associations and federations, such as the 'Venezuelan Association for an Alternative Sexual Education' and the 'Federation of Cuban Women'; (*l*) feminist groups and popular educational groups, such as the 'Popular Education Group with Women' in Mexico; 'Popular Feminine Education' in Colombia; 'Women on the March' in Puerto Rico; 'Autonomous Lesbian Feminist Mothers' in Argentina and 'The Chicana Feminist' in the United States; (*m*) documentation centres, such as the 'Networth of Documentation Centres on Women's Health' and the 'Woman and Gender Documentation Forum'.

2. *Basic premise*. The feminist and women's movement recognizes that any analysis of the situation of women must endorse the universal and interdependent nature of all human rights, including the right to development. It therefore calls on all women to struggle for these rights, putting an end to fragmentation and isolation.

3. *The situation we confront*. During the International Meeting of Solidarity among Women, 'the delegates agreed that on the eve of the Third Millennium humankind is menaced by a sort of barbarism affecting the independence of nations, the sovereignty of peoples and peace; this is the barbarism that proclaims the law of the market as the

ruler of the universe, defends privatizations and establishes free-market globalization'.[4] The participants in this meeting saw with great clarity that the present patriarchal model of neo-liberal capitalism increases poverty, diversifies economic exploitation, and multiples violence against women. Faced with this situation, the delegates stressed the need to strengthen feminist and women's movements in order to defend the interests and rights of women and counter-balance the violence done by free-market globalization.

4. *Mission.* The feminist and women's movement has as its mission the achievement of well being, of justice, of real participation, of improved quality of life, of the integral dignity and the rights of women in society and in the churches. This mission includes the establishment of bodies to forward the organization of women and to support their participation in all processes leading to sustainable development.

5. *Aim and objectives.* This movement seeks to contribute to the building of a more just society, one that prohibits any form of discrimination and violence against women. To achieve this, it maps out socio-political agendas that expose women's problems, propels socio-juridical alternatives, promote liberating cultural environments, and impact on political decision-makers.

6. *Field of action.* The tasks are carried out on a variety of levels, including: local, in urban peripheries and rural areas among women of scant means; intermediate, with representatives of popular, academic, religious, non-governmental and informational representatives and activists for social justice; national and international, with organizations, fora, networks, summits and agencies advocating women's human rights.

7. *Programmes and lines of action.* In order to carry out its mission and aims in the present situation, the movement has a wealth of programmes, areas of activity, themes and action plans, to which it is impossible to do justice in a short space. I should just like to summarize some of the activities that go to make up this qualitative and quantitative wealth. These include programmes and lines of action in: the advancement of and education in women's rights; drafting and contesting legislative proposals for women's health and reproductive rights; academic research and theoretical studies in the situation of women; documentation and publication on themes relevant to women's lives; education and professional qualification to confront and eliminate forms of violence; qualification in alternative technologies aimed at improving chances and conditions of work; publication of material in which women are both authors and subjects of the study; assessing and accompanying women's struggles in town and country; a presence on various social, pastoral, governmental, political and academic bodies so as to make women's

problems visible; participation in acts of solidarity that seek to raise the quality of women's lives.

8. *Organizational structure*. While the movement continues to debate themes related to models of the exercise of power from feminist and gender frameworks, its considered choice is for internal forms of organization that protect the exercise of democracy, solidarity and equity of opportunities and resources. So the organizations that make up the movement generally function through teams (permanent and/or voluntary) of an interdisciplinary, multilateral, intercultural and mixed-class character. These teams share the work and decisions.

Final reflections

This brief description of the women's movement is provided with the aim of inviting the world theological community and the hierarchy of individual churches to build adequate channels of conversation and dialogue with this movement. By this I mean channels constructed on bases of justice and inspired by an attitude of learning and of open accompaniment. This in turn means a dialogue free of condemnations, satanization and fear of feminist processes. Both the dominant theologies and the hierarchies of the churches are called to recognize that sexual discrimination is a sin and not a historical reality created by women. They are equally called to make specific signs of conversion and rectification through truly eliminating this discrimination.

The feminist and women's movement is a sign of hope for all Christian women and for all men who are hoping and working for a world free of violence. Its very existence witnesses to the intense activity of the Spirit of God in transforming hearts and situations from within a world of sin. Theological and ecclesial accompaniment of this movement is a human and Christian imperative if the churches wish to participate in solving the great problems that beset humankind. The creativity, wisdom and riches of this movement are good news for the churches because they show the way toward what the churches are called to be. More specifically, the Roman Catholicism of the third millennium can aspire to be 'good news' and a 'sign of hope' only to the extent that it discovers God in the faces of marginalized women, confronts the sexism that characterizes it, and initiates the course of its own transformation into a witness of its identity founded on the truth of the gospel.

Translated by Paul Burns

Notes

1. World Council of Churches, 'Ecumenical Decade Festival Concludes With Challenge To Upcoming WCC Assembly', Festival Press Release no. 5, 1, Dec. 1998.
2. http://nodo50.ix.apc.org/mujeresred/
3. http://www.nodo50.org/mujeresred/cuba.htm
4. Final document. See note 1 above.

2. Ethics

Marciano Vidal

I. Approach

Those who devote themselves to ethical reflection and moral exhortation usually begin their discourses by alluding to the crisis affecting moral values at the present time. It is indeed difficult to deny the existence of a deep moral crisis as we change centuries and millennia.[1]

Nevertheless, the following statement is also true: 'If anything is constant, it is the complaint of all ages about the prevailing immorality by comparison with earlier periods. This makes one think that we are dealing with a reiterated piece of wishful thinking that makes us exaggerate present evils and idealize what has gone before. It would be frivolous and irresponsible to say that our time is particularly immoral, any more than others in which the same was said.'[2] In the same sense, in the first third of the twentieth century the Spanish philosopher Ortega y Gasset warned against 'the plaint of decadence that snivels in the pages of so many contemporaries'.[3]

Without denying the moral crisis of the present, I shall try to view ethics as a sign of hope in our world. Pope John Paul II has given two catechetical lectures on signs of hope that, at the end of the second millennium, are apparent in both the world and the church.[4] The signs of hope transmitted by ethics are apparently tenuous, but their significance goes deep and their reach is long. They all stem from the goodness of heart of simple people, as the sub-title of these reflections indicates. Ethical hopes for the future of humankind spring from this source of goodness.

I shall allude briefly to those 'habits of heart'[5] of simple people that make up the unassailable moral nucleus on which the goodness of persons and of societies rests. These habits of goodness are expressed incomparably well in the Gospel Beatitudes (Matt. 5.3–10): the goodness of the 'poor', of the 'afflicted', of the 'dispossessed', of those who suffer 'injustice', of the 'merciful', of the 'pure in heart', of the 'peacemakers', of the 'persecuted'. Goodness in the gospel is at once a gift and a demand; this literary tension is literally underlined through the structuring of the Beatitudes into two groups, with the first four corresponding more to the 'gift' and the last four more to the task.[6] Furthermore, it is worth remembering that Christian morality is nothing more than developing and carrying out the Beatitudes.[7]

I reduce the habits of goodness of simple people, on which the ethical hopes of humankind facing the future rest, to three: clear-sightedness, to see reality without prejudices or interests; compassionate empathy, for acting in solidarity with the weak; simplicity of life, to create values alternative to the present complexity.

II. Clear-sightedness, to see reality without prejudices or interests

Ethical hope rests, in the first instance, on the capacity of simple people to 'look at' and 'see' reality without prejudices or interests. In an ethical-theological reflection on the significance of Hurricane 'Mitch', Jon Sobrino signalled the importance this natural disaster had in putting 'the weight of the real' in the forefront, that is, reality such as it is, without the distortions and memory lapses with which it is usually presented.[8] According to the Beatitude, 'Blessed are the pure in heart, for they will see God'; and in God, we might add, 'they will see human reality such as it is'.

Moral goodness is born of truth. Injustices feed on themselves through lies. When reality is 'falsified' through the numerous mechanisms available to people's minds, both as individuals and as groups, then lies become associated with evil to form the sordid world of 'alienation'. We live in an alienated world to the extent that reality is not interpreted on the basis of truth but on that of interested ideologies or ideologized interests. Alienation is nothing other than a view of reality falsified for the benefit of the 'exploiters' and to the detriment of the 'exploited'.

The greatest enemy of ethics lies in the human heart, and it has a name: the darkening of the sense of good. In the Sermon on the Mount the moral sense is compared to the 'inner eye', that which gives light to the whole person: 'The eye is the lamp of the body. So, if your eye is healthy, your whole body will be full of light; but if your eye is unhealthy, your whole body will be full of darkness. And if the light in you is darkness, how great is the darkness!' (Matt. 6.22–23). Falsification of objective reality corresponds to inner darkness. This is where the basic enemy of ethics also lurks. When prejudices, interests, ideologies and all the other forms of lie prevent us from seeing reality as it is, then it is impossible for authentic moral sensitivity and correct ethical discourse to make their appearance. It is Pope John Paul II who has most emphatically connected moral goodness with truth, above all in his encyclical *Veritatis splendor*. 'No one can elude the fundamental questions: What should I do? How can I distinguish good from evil? The reply is possible only thanks to the splendour of truth, which shines in the innermost depths of the human spirit.'[9]

Ethics stems from truth: from inner truth and objective truth. Furthermore, the first ethical imperative is, as Julián Marías pointed out so often, 'to attend to reality'. Javier Zubiri identified the 'will to truth' with the 'will to reality', and based the ethos of being human on this 'attachment to reality'. Ignacio Ellacuría, a disciple of Zubiri, developed his master's intuition. For this philosopher of liberation, one cannot be responsible by turning one's back on reality. We have to be responsible by taking on reality itself as a prime ethical imperative. This, according to Ellacuría, is divided into three stages: 1. taking stock of reality; 2. taking reality on board; 3. taking hold of reality in order to make it what it ought to be.[10] We know that this form of responsibility is so significant that the forces of evil cannot tolerate it. Faced with it, 'assassination' is the vile reaction of the powerful, while 'martyrdom' is the option taken up by those who exercise it.

There is ethical hope because there are people who live the Beatitude of the 'pure in heart'. Simple people know how to 'look' with a pure heart and are capable of 'seeing' reality such as it is. On this habit of pure heart rests the moral certitude of humankind. In the face of interested falsifications of reality, there will always be those who 'see' the suffering and unjust condition of their fellows who suffer injustice. 'I have observed the misery of my people' (Exod. 3.7).

III. Compassionate empathy, for acting in solidarity with the weak

'Clear-sightedness' leads to 'compassive empathy'. The 'pure in heart' are 'merciful' by their very nature (Matt. 5.7).

The Second Vatican Council included among the signs of the times the growing consciousness of human solidarity and its generalized acceptance: 'Among the signs of our times, the irresistibly increasing sense of solidarity among all peoples is especially noteworthy.'[11] As with its other far-reaching appreciations, the Council was not wrong in its attention to solidarity: this can become the axiological horizon of humankind at this turn of millennium. The dignity of every human person, an unassailable ethical nucleus throughout human history, now takes shape in the affirmation and striving for solidarity among individuals, among groups, among nations, and among the major areas of human experience. The great moral objective of our time is to create world solidarity.[12]

Solidarity is rooted in the consciousness of human empathy: knowing, feeling and taking on the human condition as a whole in which everyone acts in solidarity with everyone else. Hume defined empathy as the basis of ethics,[13] while Kant recognized it in his second formulation of the categorical imperative: 'Act in such a way that you use humanity, as much in your own person as in the person of anyone else, always as an end and never as a means.'[14]

This law of empathy was paradigmatically formulated in the sermon prepared by the team of Dominicans in Hispaniola (now the Dominican Republic and Haiti) and delivered by Antonio de Montesinos on the fourth Sunday of Advent 1511: 'Are these not men? Do they not have rational souls? Are you not obliged to love them as yourselves? Do you understand this, feel this? How can you be so sunk in such deep, lethargic sleep?'[15]

If empathy is the basis of solidarity, its goal is sharing. Solidarity comes about through enabling all human beings to share in the sum total of goods available. The ethical category of solidarity reveals its full significance in both the understanding of empathy and the practice of sharing. Empathy recognizes the 'other' not as a 'rival' or an 'instrument', but as an 'equal' at the unequal banquet of life. Sharing is ruled by this basic law: goods belong 'to' all and have to work 'for' all.

Ethical hope is justified by the existence of this habit of empathy in simple people. Empathic thinking is a patrimony of simple people. This emphatic thinking is based on clear-sightedness and issues in committed reason. This is what 'takes hold' of reality. Now commitment achieves its full significance when it stems from compassionate reason. No one can take hold of reality without previously 'taking stock' of it, that is, without 'weighing' it, without it 'weighing' on them in the same way it does on those affected by it.

IV. Simplicity of life, to create values alternative to the present complexity

'Simplicity' is a sign of the presence of the kingdom. 'Blessed are the poor in spirit' (Matt. 5.3). In the patristic period 'simplicity' was considered one of the signs of Christian authenticity. This simplicity is also part of the patrimony of ordinary people, whom I have called 'simple'. It makes up another habit of the heart on which ethical hope rests. 'Simplicity of life' joins with 'clear-sightedness' and 'empathy acting in solidarity' to form the nucleus of ethical hope. It is just these 'habits of heart' of ordinary people that provide the greatest human hope for the ethics of the future.

Translated by Paul Burns

Notes

1. On the contemporary moral crisis see M. Vidal, 'Crisis moral. Situación y alternativa', in *10 palabras claves en Moral del Futuro*, Estalla 1999.
2. J. Marías, *Tratado de lo mejor. La moral y las formas de vida*, Madrid 1995, 113.
3. J. Ortega y Gasset, *La rebelión de las masas*, Madrid ^{35}1995, 76.
4. Lectures given on Wednesdays 18 and 25 November 1998.
5. Cf. R. N. Bellah *et al.*, *Habits of the Heart*, New York 1988.
6. Cf. M. A. Powell, 'Matthew's Beatitudes: Reversals and Rewards of the Kingdom', *Catholic Biblical Quarterly* 58, 1996, 460–79.
7. *Catechism of the Catholic Church*, 1716–24.
8. J. Sobrino, 'La batalla de la verdad y de la compasión', *Vida nueva* 2, 166, 19/26 December 1998, 46–7.
9. *Veritatis splendor*, n. 2.
10. See, among his other writings, I. Ellacuría, *El compromiso político de la filosofía en América Latina*, Bogotá 1994.
11. *Apostolicam actuositatem*, n. 14.
12. For a development of this theme, see my *Para comprender la Solidaridad: virtud y principio ético*, Estella 1996, in which I have proposed solidarity as a new 'personal' virtue (cf. *Sollicitudo rei socialis*, 39–40) and as a new 'ethical principle' of social life (cf. *Centesimus annus*, 10).
13. D. Hume, *A Treatise of Human Nature* (numerous editions).
14. I. Kant, cited from Spanish trans., *Fundamentación de la metafísica de las costumbres*, Buenos Aires 1963, 84.
15. On the history of the composition, the impact and the handing down of this

sermon see L. Galmés, *Bartolomé de las Casas, defensor de los derechos humanos*, Madrid 1982.

16. See the Editorial, 'Fragilidad ética en el fin de siglo/milenio', in *Razón y Fe* 238, 1998, 263–8.

17. I refer the reader to F. Belo, *Lectura materialista del Evangeio de Marcos*, Estella 1975, and M. Clévenot, *Lectura materialista de la Biblia*, Salamanca 1978.

3. Greater Love, Witness to Full Life

Eduardo de la Serna

> Nothing and no one will prevent me from serving Christ and his church struggling together with the poor for their liberation. If the Lord grants me the privilege, which I do not deserve, of losing my life in this undertaking, I am at his disposition (To Fr Carlos Mugica, twenty-five years after his martyrdom, 11 May 1974)

A reflection on martyrs and martyrdom is not a flag to raise to take the cause of one who has failed on to victory. Still less is it an exercise in resentment or sorrow at the triumph of the killers and the rout of those with whom we have made common cause. Reflecting on the reality of martyrdom is purely and simply to deepen reflection into a *locus theologicus*.

Locus theologicus

Christ is, evidently, the principal reference-point of the life and death of Christians. They define themselves in terms of him. If Christians are those who follow the footsteps of the crucified and risen Nazarene, identification with him is the main criterion for reflection. This is why the tradition and liturgy of the church give such an important place to the celebration of the martyrs.

The death of Jesus, the culmination of his life spent proclaiming the good news of the kingdom to the poor, is the starting point of all reflection on martyrdom; the latter is, above all else, a christological event. Liberation theology, particularly that of Jon Sobrino and Ignacio Ellacuría, has analysed the death of Jesus and its causes in depth. A central element in their analysis is to make clear that its cause in the minds of Herod, Pilate and the Sanhedrin is one thing, while its cause in Jesus' mind is quite another. Between one and the other there is the same gulf as between hate and love. Another element to bear in mind is the reading the first Christian communities made of the event-scandal of the cross.

It would be lengthy and beside my present purpose to go deeper into this, but let me just point out some basic aspects. It is not possible to detach Jesus' death from his preaching: he was killed because of his words and his deeds; his martyrdom was the consequence of his preaching the kingdom of God. The metaphor of 'kingdom' embraces the totality of a system of universal brotherhood in which only one, God, is father. The kingdom of God is inseparable from the God of the kingdom. To call people 'brothers' and 'sisters' is intolerable for the violent, unjust, corrupt 'lords' of life and death – simply because it involves ceasing to be that. Calling God alone 'Father' is intolerable for those who believe themselves to be, and act like, 'keepers of the keys', those who presume to control – to manipulate even – God or those who prefer to place their hearts – to trust, even – in Mammon, or power. Jesus dies because he cannot deny the God whom he has preached; Jesus is killed because he does not want to abjure this God. One in the name of the God of the kingdom, the others against him: all flow together into one event – the cross.

It was the early community that found scriptural support for the Nazarene's failure in the songs of the Suffering Servant, which gave Jesus' death a new meaning as a 'death for . . . Jesus', love for his Father and for his brethren led him to death, and the communities discovered that this supreme act of love broke at root the vicious circle of violence and hate that put forward a caricature of God – an idol.

The early New Testament theologians deepened this reality of the cross by uniting it to the suffering of Christians on account of their preaching of the gospel, their persecution and martyrdom. So the importance of the theology of the cross can be seen in the Gospel of Mark; the union between Christ and the community in Matthew; the identification between the prophet of Nazareth, crucified in Jerusalem, and the passion of Stephen or Paul in Luke; the reading on two historical levels, that of Jesus and that of the Johannine community, in John.

Something similar can be said of the deutero-Pauline epistles, the First Letter of Peter, the 'letter' to the Hebrews, and the Apocalypse.

A good theology of the New Testament needs to show how this identity, especially strong in suffering and the cross, allows the followers of Jesus to be presented on the same martyrial plane. This identity also comes out in Paul's theology, in which Christians from their baptism live a life *syn Christó*, with whom they enter into close communion, to the point of sharing in his resurrection. What Archbishop Romero said on receiving his honorary doctorate in Louvain is not foreign to this historical-eschatological identification: 'Sin is what gives death to the Son of God and gives death to the children of God.'

The cross of faith and of history

The coming together of the intentions of the assassins and of the assassinated Jesus in this same happening (the cross) did, though, make it difficult to read this moment with clarity. History is full of deformed readings of the death of the Lord. The most terrible of these, on account of its present existential connotations, is that what has saved us is suffering and that pain is the redeemer of humankind. This reading, most opportune for oppressors and their accomplices, ignores the fact that what provides the gift of life that God offers is not Pilate's rage but Jesus' love. Only extreme love is the giver of full life.

This is why it seems possible, borrowing an image from christology, to speak of a cross of history and a cross of faith: a look at the cross as sin, injustice, men's violence against the unarmed prophet from Galilee, the rout of God's plan, and another dimension of the same cross, God's final word, the triumph of love over hate. In the same way that in the days of historical reading many accounts were confused by not distinguishing Jesus' life from the Christ preached as good news, so many do not distinguish sufficiently clearly between Jesus' peaceful approach (and his identification with Christians) as he moved towards a certain death and the violent approach of those who killed him. There is no doubt that the central message of the cross has to be found in love, while a dimension of sin cannot be discounted from this same cross. The witness of love 'even to death, death on a cross' given by Jesus out of fidelity to God and God's plan, must not confuse us. His Father God, the Lord of life, wanted his Son to remain faithful to the extreme of death on a cross, but he does not want injustice and sin; he wants not death but life.

Why have you forsaken me?

Reading the passion of Jesus in the 'key' of the Suffering Servant of Yahweh led the authors to cite the psalms of the just man who suffers. This dimension allows them to stress the scandal of the cross without losing its dimension of life and grace. The unjust cross, brought about by victimizers and murderers, leads believers to question the presence of God. God's forsaking of the just man who suffers at the hands of those who seem to be blessed by God provokes a crisis, a 'dark night'. 'Why have you forsaken me?' is the Psalmist's question in the face of his enemies. It is the same question as that of early Christians faced with persecution: 'Where is this God who can help the risen and cannot help the living?' It is the question of indigenous peoples faced with 'Christians' at the time of the 'conquest' of America: 'My God, where are you? Do you not hear me to come to the aid of your poor?' It is the question of the Jews in Auschwitz and of the mass of people faced with hunger, injustice and exploitation.

The sensation of God's abandonment and the apparent blessing of those who cause pain and suffering form the same *locus theologicus*: the poor as sacrament, the martyrs as witness to a greater love, both with reference to Christ, committed to people in total love, abandoned and rejected by the victimizers with the most absolute contempt.

Amor fidelium

Reflecting on Christian martyrdom is nothing other than reflecting on and making present the martyrdom of Jesus, the witness of his love.

Certain readings of the fact of martyrdom regard it as important to examine the attitude of the killers and believe that one speaks of martyrdom only in cases of *odium fidei*. This is like measuring the strength of Jesus' witness by the depth of Pilate's hatred. Removing the centre and axis of martyrdom from love, from fidelity to the kingdom of God and the God of the kingdom, is to place its centre in hatred and death and to eliminate the power of witness of martyrdom. It was certainly not hatred of the faith that made martyrs of John the Baptist or the Holy Innocents, of Maria Goretti or Edith Stein, to take just some examples. It is love of truth, of the gospel and its consequences, of the kingdom, in a word, that allows us to recognize the dimension of martyrdom in these and so many more.

It is true that if we say that those truly responsible for martyrdom are always the idols in the final analysis, these obviously absolutely reject the preaching of the kingdom of God and the God of the kingdom, and in this sense we are faced with a genuine *odium fidei*. But – and this needs saying again – it is not the idols who are responsible for Jesus being the martyr *par excellence*. They are murderers, but Jesus is martyr from love of his Father and his brethren, to which he was committed to the end. The idol of money clearly hates the followers of the God of the poor. The idol of Power hates those who choose to serve. The idol of the Market hates those who choose to share or reject profit as the motive of their lives. They cannot not hate them, because otherwise they would be destroyed. Hatred exists, certainly, hatred of the kingdom and its consequences, but it is love that counts and matters.

Commitment to the poor and their struggle for liberation, discovering and inviting others to discover brothers and sisters in others, seeking to serve and being ready to give one's life for all this, cannot be measured by the standards of those who would take our life away but only by the standards of those to whom we are committed and for whom we go on giving our lives in everyday ways. The reality of martyrdom, in short, is measured not by hatred but by love. *Magis amor fidelium quam odium fidei*.

Being Christian in Latin America

This said (and it could obviously be examined in greater depth), I have to confess my surprise at finding in Vatican documents – such as the recent Bull *Incarnationis Mysterium* (no. 13), in which is stated that 'this century now coming to an end has produced a great number of martyrs, above all through Nazism, Communism and racial or tribal conflicts' – that the reality of martyrdom in Latin America through the doctrine of National Security or 'love of money' is still ignored. It is true that the 'novelty' brought by our martyrs is that their executioners call themselves 'Christians' and that many were blessed by members of the hierarchy or nuncios, who also openly and hardly diplomatically questioned several of those who gave their lives. It is clear enough that the broadening of the term 'martyr' as proposed by Karl Rahner and, following him, such as I. Pérez del Viso and E. González, is nothing more than continuity with what the church itself has carried out in its historical praxis. As with the aboriginal inhabitants at the time of the 'conquest', self-styled 'Christians' are today responsible for killing, torturing and 'disappearing' these new martyrs. It is to be hoped that we do not have to wait another five hundred years to 'discover' the true history.

Translated by Paul Burns

4. Renewing the Face of the Earth

J. Matthew Ashley

Ever since the scientific and industrial revolutions, science and technology have elicited both glowing optimism and dark pessimism. With the fragmentation and collapse of mediaeval metaphysical and religious world-views that articulated a sense of human embeddedness in the cosmos, science emerged as the basis for a new vision of the whole and our place in it. In this cosmopolis, however, humans were abstracted from nature, and determined to be its masters.[1] Thus, science and technology went hand in hand with the tremendously optimistic sense that we are not only free, but obligated, to remake ourselves and our world. They expanded the domains in which this freedom and exigency were felt realities, an expansion that has gone under the name of 'progress' or 'development'. Science vastly extended the reach of our knowledge of the world and technology remade the face of the Earth to serve human beings – at least those fortunate enough to be born in the world's relatively wealthy enclaves. Given all this, it is not difficult to see why science and technology have exercised such a hold on our imagination and our hopes. They continue to find propagandists as enthusiastic as Francis Bacon.[2] They so deeply influence our patterns of thought that even when we worry over the deepening ecological crisis that science and technology helped to create, the solution is still conceptualized from out of this deeper world-view: sustainable development.[3]

Critics have not been slow to point out the dark side of science and technology, both as a metaphysical world-view and as a social-historical force. It is not just that new sciences like genetics have outstripped our moral wisdom, and are unleashing forces which find no other constraint than the logic of the market place. It is not just that the benefits of science and technology have devolved primarily on the wealthy nations of the world – and even there, only for certain segments of the population – while the rest are reduced to being sources to feed the ravenous maw of the scientific-technological societies of the North and cesspools for receiving their toxic wastes.[4] And here it cannot be a matter of 'developing' the rest of the globe to the technological level enjoyed by those wealthy few nations, since such a process would quickly lead to the collapse of the global biosphere, at least as one habitable by those species, like *homo sapiens*, perched precariously at the top of the food chain. What is required is what Ignacio Ellacuría called a civilization of poverty, or at least, of austerity, a goal which requires a quite different way of conceiving science and technology than as tools for analysing, manipulating and exploiting the natural world. Where will such a different conception arise? For when we attempt to grapple with these problems, as we must, we find it almost impossible to find new patterns of thought that overcome the 'environmental apartheid thinking' which segregates human beings from their environment, culture from nature.[5]

Pessimists judge that it is, in any event, already too late. The juggernaut of modernity, built with the knowledge gained through science and the power unleashed by technology, is unstoppable. We need more science, and more massive applications of technology, to solve the problems that the past science and technology helped to create. But new technologies create new problems which require in their turn new technologies, further expenditures of energy and dispersals of pollution.[6] As Edward Abbey once said, modern technological society operates with the ideology of a cancer cell, and the resultant tumour threatens to kill its host. Science and technology, as they have operated historically, and even in their much-heralded new incarnation as the 'information revolution', are not the solutions, but part of the problem. The only remaining question is whether we have gone so far that we will not be able to give up our addictions to scientific and technological 'fixes' without a collapse of the global biosphere, with horrific consequences.[7]

Optimists tell us to wait a bit longer; science and technology will yet make good on their salvific promise. Pessimists tell us that, realistically, it is already too late; we can only ride the juggernaut until it, and we with it, crash into utter ruin. But Christian hope is not optimism and Christian realism is not pessimism. Christian hope looks to an open future which is more than an extrapolation of what is. Christian realism insists that the future is not held open in the final analysis by the power of human intelligence and creativity alone, not even by science and technology. The openness of the future, which is the foundation and object of Christian hope, is a gift of God's Spirit, and manifests itself ever anew in the irruption of the kingdom of God. Insofar as science and technology are human activities which participate in that inbreaking, they are signs of hope and ought to be celebrated. What we need to ask, then, is how science and technology help us better to understand and commit ourselves to the promise and demands of this kingdom, and even to perceive new ways that the kingdom is being offered to us today, as, for instance, a kingdom composing not just human life, but the community of all living things.

Crucial to such an evaluation is overcoming the myth that human reason, paradigmatically manifested in science and technology, is and ought to be an absolutely detached observation and manipulation of reality 'from the outside'. Many twentieth-century philosophies have taken up this task. Here we might start with Ignacio Ellacuría's insight that the function of intelligence 'is not that of comprehending being or grasping meaning, but of apprehending reality and confronting ourselves with it', and that it does this as a biological activity; that is, its orientation and goal is the service of life.[8] He elaborated this insight by arguing that human intelligence includes noetic, ethical and pragmatic moments. The full actualization of human intelligence (and thus, of science and technology) certainly includes a knowledge of reality, but for Ellacuría this is not an observation and description of realities from the outside, but 'a being in the midst of the reality of things . . . which, in its active character of existing, is anything but static and thingly . . .'[9] To know reality is to find our place in reality. As such it necessarily includes an ethical moment, in which human intelligence grasps the demands that reality places upon us as that species which self-consciously participates in the ongoing history of created being.[10] Finally, human intelligence is short-circuited if it stops short of acting on that ethical imperative, if it does not lead to transformative action that participates in and contributes to the ongoing history of reality, a history that has as its ultimate goal the full realization of the kingdom of God, the holiness and glory of the indwelling of God in creation.[11]

We start then by asking how science helps us to find our place in reality. When we do, who can deny that scientific advances in this century have the potential to lead us to a deep understanding of and appreciation for reality, as well as a challenging vision of our place in it? Most importantly, twentieth-century science has definitively debunked the myth that human beings can or should be defined over and against the rest of reality. Cosmology and biology show that 'history' begins not with *homo sapiens*, but with the very origins of reality. The cosmos has a history that, just like human history, is characterized by a fascinating interplay of randomness and order, contingency and necessity, enduring structure and evanescent novelty, comedy and tragedy, dazzling moments of innovation and value and shocking displays of waste and loss.[12] Biology and the relatively new science of ecology show how interwoven human cultural, social and political economies are with the broader economy of our 'household' (*oikos*), the earth. In short, we need not wait for communications from extra-terrestrials to exclaim, 'We are not alone.' This is an advance over the classically modern view of humans as alone at the pinnacle of reality, and deserves celebration.

To the extent that ethical responsibility and action are attributes of historical being (both individual and communal), and have as their ground and *telos* right relationship within community, the ethical implications inherent to the foregoing understanding of reality are momentous. Our ethical responsibility is not confined to human history, but must be reconceived as embedded in the broader history of the cosmos. Its ground and telos is not defined just by human community, by 'culture' in abstraction from 'nature'. Rather, it finds its most fundamental horizon in the community of all created beings, particularly of organic life. This basic but crucial insight was lost with the collapse of pre-modern world-views, and is continually threatened when modernity invades so-called archaic cultures. Yet, science has the possibility of re-engendering this insight anew, on the other side of the 'disenchantment of the world'.

That scientists have begun to experience this awakening to the ethical implications intrinsic to science can be seen in the increasing role they have played as advocates for broader communities of life, both human and non-human. A milestone in this awakening was passed in 1945, when a number of scientists involved in the Manhattan Project banded together to urge that the United States give up its nuclear monopoly, that nuclear weapons be banned, and that nuclear energy be placed at the service of the entire human community. *The Bulletin of the Atomic Scientists*, with its famous 'doomsday clock', resulted, and although the 'Atomic Scientists of Chicago' were brushed aside by the US military and government at the time, they have nonetheless constituted a potent force for realizing more fully the ethical–political dimension that is inherent to science.

It is in the third dimension of human intelligence, the realization of human intelligence in action, that most still remains to be done, partly because technology is not simply the praxis-dimension of science alone. During the industrial and information revolutions it became thoroughly integrated into capitalist economic systems fixed on development, production and consumption. In this context technology entails the one-way reconfiguration of nature for the purposes of a society defined by those processes. Yet, the only coherent continuation of the rational and ethical insights found in contemporary science – as opposed to the science that prevailed during modern capitalism's birth in the seventeenth and eighteenth centuries – is the creative reconfiguration of society and nature together, for the sake of a sustainable community of all life on earth.[13]

The signs of hope that are to be found here come when technology participates in the option for the poor, since it is among the poor that the death-dealing shortcomings of our present technological order are most evident. The most striking and innovative instance of this is manifested in the development of 'appropriate technologies', which, in accordance with the principle of subsidiarity, meet human needs at the lowest possible level of organization, and with the least environmental impact.[14] This does not render rigorous and cutting-edge research in science and engineering superfluous, but gives them new scope and new challenges. True, developing a dry-composting toilet or more efficient solar cells may lack the drama of damming the Yangtze River or building the next generation of computers (and is less profitable for large corporations). Yet, the underlying insight that the only sustainable and just future lies in tapping into and co-operating with renewable energy flows rather than in profligately expending our limited sources of nonrenewable energy, defines a strategy that requires just as much scientific acumen and engineering finesse.

There is both hope and challenge to be found in the scientific and technological advances of this century. The hope is for a new cosmopolis, an integration of humans and their world into a community which is a sacrament manifesting and celebrating a God of life. Science and technology can and should remain central to such a community, but they can do so only when the sense of mystery, indeed of the sacred, that is implicit to our scientific vision of reality is made explicit and then informs our technology.[15] Therein lies the challenge, for scientists and believers alike: neither a blind embrace of science and technology, nor their demonization and rejection, but a recognition of the diverse ways (scientific, technological, religious) that we can and must let ourselves be grasped by that Spirit of life who renews the face of the Earth.

Notes

1. On the role of science in the forging of a modern 'cosmopolis', see Stephen Toulmin, *Cosmopolis: The Hidden Agenda of Modernity*, New York 1990, *inter alia*, 67–80, 98–117.

2. See, for instance, Edward O. Wilson's unapologetic apology for Enlightenment science, *Consilience: The Unity of Knowledge*, New York 1998.

3. This term is used without seriously asking whether it is not finally an oxymoron. For a trenchant critique, see Larry Rasmussen, *Earth Community, Earth Ethics*, Maryknoll, NY 1996, 127–73.

4. For an overview, see Bryan Massingale, 'An Ethical Reflection upon "Environmental Racism"' in *The Challenge of Global Stewardship: Roman Catholic Responses*, ed. Maura A. Ryan and Todd David Whitmore, Notre Dame, In. 1997, 234–50.
5. See Rasmussen, *Earth Community, Earth Ethics* (n. 3), 31–4, 77–83.
6. For a classic and unrelievedly pessimistic evaluation of this sort see Jacques Ellul, *The Technological Society*, New York 1964.
7. And, of course, some argue that we are already in the midst of such a collapse. See, for example, Robert D. Kaplan, 'The Coming Anarchy: Nations Break Up under the Tidal Flow of Refugees from Environmental and Social Disaster', *Atlantic Monthly* 273/2, February 1994.
8. Ignacio Ellacuría, 'Hacia una Fundamentación del Método Teológico Latinoamericano', *Liberación y Cuativerio: Debates in Torno al Metodo de la teología en America Latina*, ed. Enrique Ruíz Maldonado, Mexico City 1975, 624.
9. Ibid., 626.
10. Ellcuría calls this dimension of human intelligence 'shouldering the weight of reality' (*el cargar con la realidad*), ibid.
11. See Jürgen Moltmann, *The Coming of God: Christian Eschatology*, London and Minneapolis 1996, 306–19.
12. For two attempts to render this dimension of our scientific understanding of nature clear, see Langdon Gilkey, *Nature, Reality, and the Sacred: The Nexus of Science and Religion*, Minneapolis 1993, especially Part 2; and Brian Swimme and Thomas Berry, *The Universe Story: From the Primordial Flaring Forth to the Ecozoic Era – A Celebration of the Unfolding of the Cosmos*, San Francisco 1992.
13. See Rasmussen, *Earth Community, Earth Ethics* (n. 3), 53–74.
14. See Albert J. Fritsch, SJ, 'Appropriate Technology and Healing the Earth', in *Embracing Earth: Catholic Approaches to Ecology*, ed. Albert LaChance and John Carroll, Maryknoll, NY 1994, 96–115.
15. Many scientists recognize this. See Carl Sagan, Hans Bethe et al., 'An Open Letter to the Religious Community', cited in Rasmussen, *Earth Community, Earth Ethics* (n. 3), 183, 245.

A Total Jubilee: 'Giving Hope to the Poor and Receiving It from Them'

Jon Sobrino

Every fifty years Israel proclaims good news to the poor: remission of debts, return of land, freedom from slavery . . . And today too, on the occasion of the jubilee year of 2000, many people are insisting on the same: remission of external debt, achieving the promised aid level of 0.7 per cent of GNP . . . So the jubilee is good news for the poor (not for creditors and landlords), just as the 'kingdom of God proclaimed by Jesus' is (not for profiteers and oppressors) and the resurrection of Jesus, in which 'God does justice to a victim' (not to an executioner, or even simply to a corpse). There is, then, an essential relationship between poor (victims, crucified peoples) and hope of good news, and outside this relationship the idea of jubilee makes no sense. I should like to reflect on this in this article, but if our human race – all of it – wants to celebrate the jubilee, it is not only the poor who should receive good news 'from us', but we, in our turn, should be ready to receive it 'from them'. This idea, unfamiliar in many quarters, is central in the thought of Archbishop Romero and Ignacio Ellacuría. So for the North to remit the external debt of the poor countries would be a jubilee, but it would also be a jubilee for the North to allow itself to be forgiven and humanized by the South. This the total jubilee indicated by the title of this article.

I. The situation of the poor: the jubilee as a question of honesty, faith and praxis

(a) Without naïveté: jubilee as protest

Each year the United Nations report unmasks the complacency of our world. There is a gigantic scandal: two-thirds of the human race live in poverty and 1,300,000,000 have to live on less than a dollar a day – 'the macro-blasphemy', as Pedro Casaldáliga calls it. So there is an immense moral sin, because it deals death. A grave sin, because of 'the immense weight of the economic system' (Luis de Sebastián). In its present free-market form, this sin is furthermore 'the vengeance of the rich, the cynical triumph of the traditional elites' (Jose Comblin). And to complete the picture, one must add the current disillusion: neither generosity, nor solidarity, nor holiness, nor martyrdom, nor revolutions seem to bring the poor justice or dignity or brotherhood. Sin, then, 'is in power', and so it would be good for this jubilee to resound with protest. Either in the form of theo-dicy (on which Metz insists) and/or in the form of anthropo-dicy, cries and shouts have to resound, like those of the Israelites in Egypt or those of Jesus on the cross. Without these cries we shall not be celebrating a real jubilee but a docetist one: the good news proclaimed will not be dialectical and confrontational, as it is in scripture, but co-optable.

(b) Without cynicism: jubilee in the midst of grace

No naïveté, then, but also no cynicism, *hybris* in the ultimate sense, to prevent us from accepting the grace that also exists in our world. There are struggles for justice and struggles to 'incorporate' into existence those at present 'excluded' from it. And the struggle goes on in the churches, to prevent them from succumbing to dehumanization, to the inconsequence of saying that human rights are one thing outside the church and another inside it, to inculcating fear rather than joy, to being frightened of finding Jesus come back to this world in the martyrs . . .

There are successes too. Pinochet has not had the last say on his victims, nor are the generals of Guatemala the final guardians of the memory of a people. There is something in good that does not die, as expressed in these words of Ann Manganaro, a religious doctor who worked with peasants in Chalatenango: 'Seeing their faces, listening to their stories, my heart could not but be sorrowful. But I am not sad. I find myself learning from these people what I had always hoped would be true: that love is stronger than death.' We never uproot the gospel wholly from our history, and many go on putting it into practice.

This final wager for good has been elaborated – scandalously and salvifically – in the Christian faith, right from the outset. There is no equality between grace and sin, but the presumption is always in favour of good. 'Where sin abounded, grace superabounded' (Paul); 'God broke for ever the symmetry of being either possibly saviour or possibly sentencer. God is, in essence, saviour' (Karl Rahner). And Ignacio Ellacuría wrote these historic and provocative words on salvation: 'From my point of view – and this may be something at once prophetic and paradoxical – the United States is in a far worse state than Latin America. Because the United States has a solution, but, in my view, it is bad solution, both for itself and for the world in general . . . In Latin America there are no solutions, only problems; but, however painful this may be, it is better to have problems than to have a bad solution for the future of history.'[1] Paradox? Certainly, but no greater than others we repeat in the liturgy with no problem (since in the liturgy we run little risk, and the crude reality of the poor is not present): 'Who will separate us from the love of Christ? . . . neither death, nor life, nor angels, nor rulers, not things present, nor things to come, nor powers' (cf. Rom. 8. 35–39). 'That the hope of the poor will not perish' is a statement as final and utopian as Paul's.

(c) The present conflict: the battle for the hope of the poor

Besides the presence of grace and sin, the present-day world is the site of a great battle, a decisive one for the poor and one in which all who celebrate the jubilee must take part: this is the battle for the hope of the poor. 'Official' pronouncements can function perfectly well without the least mention of this hope. It is possible to proclaim 'the end of history' (Francis Fukuyama), with the implication that there is nothing further to hope for. The market can be presented as the gospel already realized with the World Bank as its evangelist (Maurice Camdessus). And so that not even the saving power of the cross can be applied to the poor and the victims, the modern business corporation can be presented as the figure of the suffering servant of Yahweh, an incarnation of God's presence in this extremely undervalued world (Michael Novak). So today it is possible to express the good news without mentioning the poor and their hope. This is of no concern: if it surfaces, it has to be destroyed, and to prevent it from even surfacing we pursue 'the geo-politics of despair and inevitability' (Xavier Gorostiaga) and throw in the TINA syndrome: 'There is no alternative'.

A campaign against the hope of the poor has been launched. And for good reasons, since this hope – that 'we can live in a different manner' – is the greatest threat to the world of abundance, as Nelson Rockefeller well realized on his tour of Latin America thirty years ago. But others do not see things in this way, and the best always struggle for this hope. In the midst of repression and death, Oscar Romero declared: 'I, full of hope, not only in God but in human beings, say: "Yes, there is a way out".' And Ignacio Ellacuría, a few months before his martyrdom, said that we have to turn history back, and to do so together with all the poor and oppressed, utopically and full of hope.

The hope of the poor is, then, a threat to some and salvation to others.

The jubilee of 2000, an occasion of celebration as it should be, should also be a symbol of this primordial conflict in our present-day world: what is to become of hope. And the problem is a serious one, because, as Pedro Casaldáliga says, 'If you take a people's hope away, you have taken everything'. The struggle for this hope might well be the central praxis guiding the jubilee celebrations. It would be the 'orthopraxis' to accompany the utopic 'orthodoxy' of the psalmist: 'the hope of the poor [shall not] perish forever' (Ps. 9.19). The conclusion is that celebrating the jubilee requires honesty about the situation, faith in the possibility of grace, and praxis to decide the great battle for hope in favour of the poor.

II. The root of hope; the good news of God brought by Jesus

Let us now look at the sap on which the jubilee lives and at what Christianity positively has to offer so that 'the hope of the poor [shall not] perish for ever'. The basic fact is that, between joys and protests, the Christian faith holds as central and immutable truth that God is good news, and has been shown as such in Jesus: in this land of sin, suffering and death a good reality has appeared. Put in theological language, 'the grace of God has appeared, bringing salvation to all' (Titus 2.11); put in christological language, Jesus 'went about doing good and healing all who were oppressed' (Acts 10.38); put in anthropological language, 'a single shared table'.

(a) Jesus' proclamation

Jesus' good news is the proclamation of life and dignity, of the end of misfortunes for the poor, for those who do not count, those who have no voice (*neipoi*) – who in the time of Jesus could be grouped into these four categories: the poor, for whom living is a heavy burden; the sick; sinners/ publicans; women. In this world, Jesus announces that 'the kingdom of God has come near' (Mark 1.14), frees them from stifling oppressions, particularly religious: 'My yoke is easy, and my burden is light' (Matt. 11.30), and gives them back self-esteem and dignity in the face of contempt: 'Your faith has made you well; go in peace' (Mark 5.34; Luke 7.50). And, most significant in a religious society, he allows and encourages sinners and publicans to say simply: 'Abba, beloved Father'. In short, Jesus brought good news, and so 'people came to him from every quarter' (Mark 1.45).

From this we can draw a further important conclusion, because it radicalizes the good news. We have to make the poor the subject of the ethical praxis of the churches, certainly, but for Jesus they are much more: they are a theo-logal reality. The kingdom of God is for the poor ('only for them', says Jeremias) by the mere fact of their being poor, which makes the poor appear in a strict relationship with God, as Puebla – in unheard-of terms – repeats: 'The poor deserve preferential attention, whatever the moral or personal situation they find themselves in. Made in the image and likeness of God to be his children, this image is darkened and even mocked. This is why God takes up their defence and loves them' (no. 1142). This text, composed by the bishops of Latin America, today seldom cited and virtually buried, expresses the Jesus principle and should be central to the jubilee: the poor, theologal realities, speak to us of God.

(b) Closeness to the end

Jesus' fate was also very soon seen as good news. Suffice to recall that both Paul and John interpret the cross as love and salvation, so good news. Nevertheless, we should – and in my view must – introduce the poor of this world into the pasch as a central element, and also, rather than see them as simply poor, call them 'victims', or 'crucified peoples'. In the cross of Jesus, victims see failure and loss for themselves on the one hand, since it does not show power, the otherness hoped for from the Messiah and his God (so different from the powerlessness of the poor) that could bring them salvation. But on the other hand they see affinity in the cross, closeness to their own situation – and this is already an expression of love, of salvation. On the cross, love seems powerless, but for the poor it is at least credible.

In the resurrection God's power does appear, but not directly, in universal form, nor is its purpose simply to demonstrate God's omnipotence. God gives life back not simply to a dead body, but to a crucified one; God does justice to a victim. What is good news about the resurrection is not, therefore, the proclamation of a life beyond death (which the Egyptians and the Greeks also hoped for), but hope for victims: that the executioner will not triumph over them. Jesus' pasch is, then, good news; but it is directly so for victims – another lesson that we should not forget in the jubilee.

(c) A good man

Jesus is also good news in a third sense of *eu-aggelion*, one that, unlike the preceding ones, is not often taken into account. If we ask what attracted the attention of the poor people who 'came to him from every quarter', the answer has to be his proclamation of the kingdom and the liberating actions that accompanied it: healings, casting out of demons, welcoming sinners and outcasts, praxis of denouncing and unmasking the powerful and oppressors . . . But the sort of person Jesus was and the way he acted also made a great impact on them.

In Jesus they saw someone who spoke with authority, without hidden meanings, convinced of what he said. In their troubles, they flocked to him with this simple request: 'Lord, have mercy on me'. Children, of whom little notice was taken, were not afraid of him, and women, who were despised, kept him company. The crowds of ordinary people were so close to him that at the end of his life he found his greatest protection in them – which is why he had to be seized 'by night and through betrayal'. The poor found in Jesus someone who loved them and defended them, simply because they were poor. And this made a great impression on them. Jesus, then, was 'good news' – and in its primary sense – also through the way he behaved and acted. In this – even before the believing experience of the pasch – lies the original experience of good news: the reality of a good Jesus who went about doing good, to which the response was orthopathy, letting oneself be affected by him in the right way. Again, the church would do well to remember this: it will give hope to the poor only through being and acting like Jesus.

(d) Grace and truth

All that the Synoptics affirm descriptively is set out systematically in John's Prologue. The whole of this (and the Prologue to 1 John) is shot through with good news. By this I mean that he is not proclaiming a truth – which turns out to be good news – but directly announcing good news, which is then held to be true. These are not mutually contradictory, but the emphasis is different. Read in this way, the Prologue says that in this world of darkness, death and provisionality – including Moses and John the Baptist – light, life and definitiveness have appeared: we can be sons and daughters of God. This is true, but it is first, logically, good news.

The Prologue also specifies what this good news consists of: *charis kai aletheia* (v. 17), grace and truth. The 'good news' is put before the 'truth', and this is supported by the way the gospel speaks of the evil one: he is a 'murderer and father of lies', in that order. And the good news is partial: the fullness received is *ḥesed*, God's compassion, with the connotation of partiality and tenderness to the poor.

In the Jubilee, the churches would do well to 'pitch their tent' in the *sarx* of this world, and to take *charis kai aletheia* to it. And they would be well advised to place the good news first. Pope John XXIII described the church as *Mater et magistra*, mother and teacher – in that order. Ignacio Ellacuría did the same: 'The maternal character of the church expresses what it has of bearer of humanity and of sanctity, of bearer of new impulses and ideas bringing liberation . . . If the church is configured as people of God more by its maternal powers than its magisterial ones, it will be in a better position to make its contribution to the liberation of humankind and of history.'²

III. The good news today: witnesses and shared table

(a) Witnesses

What is it that makes Jesus go on being good news to the poor today? Is there something 'metaparadigmatic' in Jesus that goes on giving hope to the poor of this world? The reply is a decided Yes, which I would summarize as follows:

– What makes Jesus' impact in his mercy and the primacy he accords it: there is nothing before or after this, and from this he defines the truth of both God and human beings.

– What makes his impact is his honesty with reality and his will to truth, his judgment on the oppressed majorities and the oppressing minorities: being a voice of the voiceless and a voice against those who have too much voice.

– What makes his impact is his fidelity in upholding honesty and justice to the end against internal crises and external persecutions.

– What makes his impact is his freedom in blessing and cursing, in going to the synagogue on the sabbath and violating the sabbath, the absolute freedom of allowing nothing to stand in the way of doing good.

– What makes his impact is his acceptance of sinners and outcasts, sitting at table and feasting with them, rejoicing that God is revealed in them.

– What makes his impact are his – modest – signs of the kingdom and his utopian vision, taking in the whole of society and history.

– Finally, what makes Jesus' impact is his trust in a good and close God, whom he calls Father, and the fact that in turn he opens himself to a Father who is still God, a mystery that cannot be manipulated.

– And what makes his greatest impact is that he does simultaneously so many things that are difficult to combine. That is what gladdens the hearts of the poor.

People like this have surfaced throughout history. In Oscar Romero the people rejoiced in having a good archbishop, one who proclaimed the kingdom and denounced idols, but also one who was good. His manner, close and compassionate, was in itself *eu-aggelion*. And it is this aspect, and impossible to understand without it, that makes the impact of his death and his 'rising again in the Salvadorean people', as he prophesied. His pasch was also seized on as *eu-aggelion*. And so it is with others:

Martin Luther King, Dietrich Bonhoeffer, Simone Weil, Dorothy Day . . . to name some of the better known. And there are others, the vast majority, little known, who throughout history have kept alive the good news that Jesus was. 'Being human is a defective mode of being Christ', Rahner said – to which I would add 'ways of being good news'.

(b) The shared table

The good news of the person, mission and destiny of Jesus has also taken social shape throughout the course of history, and its best expression is 'the shared table'. This began with Jesus himself, sharing a table with the poor and sinners, publicans and women of easy virtue. Paul dreamed of one table for Jews and Gentiles, free persons and slaves, men and women. This shared table, the good news that has to be proclaimed to the poor today, is the symbol of a new civilization, one that can truly humanize. I would describe its basic characteristics, positively and dialectically, in the following terms:

– It is a civilization of community as opposed to isolating individualism which degenerates into egoism; of celebration as opposed to mere irresponsible amusement, which can be industrialized and commercialized and degenerates into alienation; of openness to others as opposed to cruel ethnocentrism, which degenerates into indifference to the sufferings of others and despising them; of creativity as opposed to lazy copying and servile imitation, which degenerates into loss of one's own identity.

– It is a civilization of commitment as opposed to mere tolerance, which degenerates into indifference; of the spirit of justice as opposed to sheer aid, which covers up the world's tragedy; of solidarity as opposed to the independent-mindedness of those who need no one, even if they end up alone.

– It is a civilization of the spirit of truth as opposed to propaganda and lies, on which reality takes revenge sooner or later; of memory and remembrance as opposed to forgetting, which degenerates into impunity for evildoers and neglect of the victims.

– It is a civilization of faith as opposed to dull positivism and pragmatism, which lead to a meaningless life; of a church of the poor as opposed to a falsely universal church, one of all, which supports the powerful.

– Finally, it is a civilization of utopia as opposed to disillusion, even if this utopia is so simple – and so positive and so misplaced – as that life may be possible.

IV. The good news that comes from the poor

I began this article by saying that the jubilee has to work in two ways. So far I have dealt with what it brings to the poor. I should now like to conclude with a brief look at two ways in which poor can bring the jubilee to us.

(a) The true civilization that comes from the world of poverty

In his last years, Ignacio Ellacuría worked out the idea of a 'civilization of poverty', a phrase so provocative that others re-formulated it as 'civilization of shared austerity'. But Ellacuría insisted on the original because the present civilization of wealth (and of the priority of capital over labour) has not only failed to solve the basic problem of life but has not civilized humankind either. It has not made the shared table possible but has blessed the table of Dives and Lazarus. It is not to be hoped that the human will come 'from above', 'out of abundance', 'from the industrialized democracies'; it can come only 'from below'. So he trusted in the 'civilization of poverty' in this dialectical, prophetic and utopian sense. It is from this viewpoint that one can understand that the poor are, without doubt, those who offer the best chance of a shared table. This is not a mechanical process, since the mystery of evil certainly dwells in them too (and, in times of war, repression or disasters can appear with terrifying force, leading them to destroy one another). But – and in a seemingly natural way – there is something in the world of poverty that brings a humanizing process that does not exist, or not in the same way, in the world of abundance. The world of poverty therefore functions as a sacrament of humanization – paradoxically and scandalously. It is the world of the servant of Yahweh, in which God dwells – often hidden and disfigured but also often obvious and welcoming. To build the shared table, it will be a great help to begin with this world of poverty, and this – again – is something we should take note of in the jubilee.

(b) The pardon granted by victims

Let me end by taking up what is specific to the biblical jubilee: the remission of debts. In 2000 we must 'cancel the debts of the poorest', as many agree, with Pope John Paul II taking the lead. But 'who will remit the debts of the rich and the oppressors, who will repair the damage they have inflicted on the poor?' The jubilee refers to Leviticus, in which the debts the poor have contracted are written off. But for it to be a total jubilee we also need to refer to the songs of the Servant, according to which the oppressive world is the one that produces victims and so contracts an absolutely grave and unjust debt with them.

Can this 'debt' be pardoned? And who will pardon it? Sometimes 'bastard jubilees' are celebrated in order to pardon oppressors and executioners through unjust legislation or insulting amnesties. But sometimes pardon is genuine; it is granted by the victims. And on this note I should like to end. This is what happened in the 1980s in a shelter in San Salvador on the commemoration of All Souls: 'Around the altar that day were several placards with the names of relatives who had been killed and assassinated, with flowers around their names. Next to these placards were others without flowers, saying simply: "Our dead enemies. May God forgive them and convert them." When the eucharist was over, an old man explained to us what the placards meant: "We made these placards as if we were going to put flowers on our dead, since in that way it seemed to us that they would feel we were with them. But as we are Christians – you know? – we thought that they too, the enemies, should be on the altar, although we didn't dare put flowers on them. They are our brothers in spite of killing and murdering us. You know what the Bible says: it's easy to love your own people, but God also asks us to love those who persecute us."'

This is a moving account, without a doubt, but also an enlightening one. The poor are often open to forgiving, and so the basic problem is another: for the rich and powerful of this world to let themselves be forgiven, to accept the pardon offered them by the victims – something not done by oligarchs, generals and politicians in Third World countries, nor by economies, banking systems and military regimes throughout the world. The most urgent question for the jubilee is to make life possible for the poor (which means writing off their so-called debts). But the deeper problem, and harder to solve, is for the North to allow itself to be forgiven by the South, which will then enable it to turn more decidedly to the poor and to make the shared table possible. Utopia? Certainly, but a utopia we must work for, because only in this way can we celebrate a total jubilee and only then will it be possible to make a shared table of this world.

Translated by Paul Burns

Notes

1. 'Quinto centenario de América Latina. ¿Descubrimiento o encubrimiento?', *Revista Latinoamericana de Teología* 21, 1990, 277.
2. 'Liberación', ibid. 30, 1993, 228ff.

IV · Closing Reflections

Jubilee Litanies

Pedro Casaldáliga

Opening Prayer

God of love, our Father, our Mother:
In the midst of this humanity, all of it your daughter, we who are the church of Jesus feel the need to ask your pardon and at the same time give you thanks as we complete these two thousand years of Christianity in history and in the hope of a new millennium more worthy of your heart and of humankind itself.

We ask this for all those men and women who throughout these twenty Christian centuries have honoured the gospel with their lives and perhaps even their deaths, and in the name of all the poor of the earth, for whom the gospel of your kingdom should be Good News Indeed.

Litany of Contrition

The Response is: **Awaken our memory and renew our hearts.**

For having taken exclusive control of your name, and for not having recognized you in other religions;

For the self-sufficiency and self-importance of our worship and for the narrow fundamentalism with which we have interpreted your message in the Bible;

Because we have not known how to discover and proclaim the maternal side of your face;

For the ethnocentricity, colonialism and Westernization of our faith;

Because in your name and appealing to your Word we have destroyed so much Word breathing in the books, temples, monuments and celebrations of aboriginal cultures;

Because throughout these twenty centuries we have condemned as paganism what we failed to understand, on account of our fundamentalist and proselytizing faith;

For the many wars of religion we have embarked on, invoking your name and brandishing your cross;

For the unjustifiable timidity of our ecumenical efforts, often reduced to sporadic services and verbal promises without daring to live communion in faith, eucharist and service as you would wish;

For the evangelization we have carried out on the arm of empires and armies in America, Asia and Africa;

Because we have so often handed down as your message what was in fact a dominant culture;

For the worldly titles, for the insulting luxury, in the structures and life of so many church bodies;

Because we have so often blessed armies and conquests, crusades and dictators;

Because, even though we too are descended from Abraham in faith, we have cultivated so much anti-Semitism and anti-Islamism, and have made the birthplace of Jesus a land of conquests and hatreds;

Because we made justification, the pure gift of your love, a wounding division in the church;

Because, between reforms and counter-reforms, we have not known how to carry out true reform of the church *semper reformanda*;

Because in the name of a short-sighted orthodoxy and an all-embracing power without pluralism or mercy we have been capable of committing the horrors of the Inquisition, and of condemning prophecy, theology and public opinion in the church;

Because, denying the innovative witness of Jesus, we have so marginalized women in society and in the church, silencing them, subjecting them, and even fanatically burning them as witches;

For our connivance and participation, or silence and justification, in the enslavement of your black people, sometimes in the name of the Bible itself;

For our minds closed to acceptance of the autonomy of history, and of science and technology, and for our fear of 'modern freedoms';

Because we have not known how to grasp the option for the poor as the heart of the gospel, because we have long colluded with capitalism and still fail to protest at the exclusions brought about by the 'free market';

For racism and ethnic cleansing; for ecocide and hunger; for holocausts, gulags, scorched earth policies, disappearings, personnel mines; for absentee landlords, shanty towns, unemployment; for assaults on human dignity and that of minorities – in all of which we have so often taken part through omission, indifference, or even complicity, throughout these twenty centuries.

A Litany of Thanksgiving and Hope

The Response is: **We sing your love and adopt your kingdom.**

Because we believe you are love and community; because we believe you took flesh in our history; because we know you as God-with-us;

Because throughout the history of Christianity there have always been true followers of Jesus, witnesses to your kingdom;

For the unnumbered legion of our sisters and brothers in faith who have sealed their fidelity with the greatest proof of martyrdom, yesterday and today, under all powers and against all lies;

Because the Bible, your word, is at last increasingly in the hearts and the hands of the people;

Because the option for the poor is being shown to us anew as the gospel paradigm of the life and mission of the church;

For the witness of the early communities and the often heroic endurance of evangelical communities even in the most authoritarian periods of the church, and for the new flowering of base church communities;

Because theology has been able to study you over the centuries, even when faced with incomprehension, and for the new theologies – political, liberation, black, feminist, ecological – engaged in generous dialogue with the many-sided reality of new human struggles;

For the ecumenism faithful to the testament of Christ that is making its way in the churches, already an irreversible and growing process, Jesus' dream 'that the world may believe';

For the inter-faith dialogue and macro-ecumenical experiences that are at last taking shape on so many frontiers of your human family;

For the women and men, known and unknown, prophets of peace, witnesses to human rights, heralds of utopia, who keep alive our hope and the beauty of your presence;

Because we have finally discovered inculturation as essential to true evangelization;

For the emergence of the laity, especially women, and their presence and participation in the life and services of the church;

For the flowering of religious spirit in a world that has sometimes declared you dead, and for the new Pentecostal presence of your Spirit;

For the signs of renewal of church structures, proclaiming, not long off, a co-responsible and co-equal church, organic and free, harmoniously one and many;

For many witnesses to religious life living on the peripheries and frontiers of society;

For the victories of the indigenous cause and the black cause;

For the volunteer spirit of young people, for their conscientious objection and opposition to militarism;

Because we are finally coming to an understanding and experience of ecology, feeling co-responsible for the mysteries of the universe;

For human rights, increasingly claimed as divine rights;

For the new rights of people vindicated in alternative courts of law, workplaces and other organizations;

For all the aspects of solidarity shown between the First World and the Third World;

Because a world-wide solidarity and sharing are developing in the face of the globalization of profit and market;

For the new possibilities in communication, for advances in medicine and science in general in the service of human health and happiness;

Because despite the powers of darkness and the dark night of the poor in this global market place, we still dream and struggle and have not lowered the standard of utopia, and life conquers death, and you, the living God who raised Jesus, Father and Mother of the whole human family, are still our future, glorious for ever.

Translated by Paul Burns

Contributors

LEONARDO BOFF, one of the founding fathers of liberation theology, was born in 1938 and for many years taught systematic theology at the Franciscan Institute in Petrópolis. He is now Professor of Ethics at the State University of Rio de Janeiro. The author of over sixty books, many of them translated in English, his recent works deal with ecology and include *Ecologia; Grito da Terra, Grito dos Pobres* (1995; Eng. trans. 1997); *A nova era: a civilizão planetária* (1997); *A águia e a galinha: uma metáfor a da condicião humana* (1998); *Saber cuidar: ethos do humano e compaxião de Terra* (1999).

Address: C.P. 92144, Petrópolis 27541, RJ, Brazil.

ELIZABETH AMOAH is Senior Lecturer in the Department for the Study of Religions, University of Ghana, Legon, Ghana.

Address: The University of Ghana, Department for the Study of Religions, P.O. Box 66, Legon, Accra, Ghana.

CARLOS MENDOZA ÁLVAREZ was born in Puebla de los Ángeles in Mexico in 1961. A Dominican friar, he studied at the Dominican *studium* in Mexico City and then read philosophy at the National Autonomous University of Mexico and the Institut Catholique in Paris before taking a doctorate in theology at the university of Fribourg. He has founded theological courses in Mexico and Chile as well as taking part in starting and editing two reviews. He is Dominican regent of studies in Mexico City and lectures in theology at the Pontifical University of Mexico. He has published *Deus liberans*, a study of Christian revelation in dialogue with modernity (1996), and contributed to *Los desafíos contextuales de la teología latinoamericana* (1997) and *Secularidad y cultura contemporánea: desafíos para la teología* (1998).

Address: Aguascalientes 16, Roma Sur, 06760 Mexico, DF.
E-mail: carlosme@infosel.net.mx

JOHN MANNION was born in Ireland in 1934, studied at the local schools and later at a diocesan secondary school, and matriculated in 1953. He worked as a labourer in England for five years before entering the seminary. Ordained in 1966, he graduated from the University of Leicester with a Bachelor of Science degree (1971) and taught in secondary schools in England until 1984. He wrote on the meaning of religious life in 'Supplement to Doctrine and Life' (1976 approx.), studied Spanish and went to work in Nicaragua, 1985–1987, then came to the United States where he is pastor of a suburban parish in the Archdiocese of San Antonio.

Address: 5667 Old Pearsall Road, San Antonio, TX 78242–2335, USA.

ENRICO CHIAVACCI was born in Siena in 1926 and ordained priest in 1950. He studied engineering at the University of Florence and theology at the seminary there, and also in Rome and Naples, gaining a doctorate. He is Emeritus Professor of Moral Theology in the Theological Faculty of Central Italy, based in Florence, and also President of the 'Justice and Peace Commission' of the Archdiocese of Florence. His main books are *La Gaudium et spes. Commento analitico*, Rome 1967; *Morale della vita fisica*, Bologna 1975; *Theologia Morale* (4 vols), Assisi 1977–1990; and *Invito alla teologia morale*, Brescia 1997.

Address: Parrochia S. Silvestro, Via di Ruffignano 10, I 50141 Firenze, Italy.

JOSÉ-IGNACIO GONZÁLEZ FAUS was born in Valencia in 1933. He is a Jesuit and teaches systematic theology in the Catalonia Faculty. He is Academic Director of the 'Christianity and Justice' study centre in Barcelona. His many publications include *La Humanidad nueva. Ensayo de Cristología* (1994); *La libertad de palabra en la Iglesia y la teología* (trans. into English as *Where the Spirit Breathes*); *Vicarios de Cristo. Los pobres en la teología y la espiritualidad cristianas*; *La lógica del reinado de Dios*. His most recent works are *La autoridad de la verdad. Momentos oscuros del magisterio eclesiástico* (1996) and *Fe en Dios y construcción de la historia* (1998).

Address: Centre Borja, Llaseres 30, Sant Cugat del Valle (Barcelona), Spain.

ELSA TAMEZ, born in Mexico in 1950, holds degrees in theology, literature and linguistics and a doctorate of theology from the university of Lausanne. She is Rector of the Seminario Bíblico Latinoamericano in Costa Rica and belongs to the Ecumenical Theological Education committee of the World Council of Churches as well as being a moderator of the Ecumenical Association of Third World Theologians and a theological assessor for the Latin American Council of Churches. Her published books include a Concise Greek–Spanish Dictionary, *La Biblia de los Oprimidos* (1979; Eng. trans. *The Bible of the Oppressed*); *Santiago, una lectura latinoamericana de la epístola* (1985; Eng. trans. *St James. A Latin American Reading of the Epistle*); *Contra toda condena* (1990; Eng. trans. *Against All Condemnation*). She has edited four other books, mainly of feminist theology, and contributed articles to *Concilium* and other theological journals.

Address: Universidad Bíblica Latinoamericana, Calle 3, Avenidas 14 y 16, Apdo. 901–1000, San José, Costa Rica, CA.

DAVID N. POWER, OMI, is Professor of Systematic Theology and Liturgy at The Catholic University of America, Washington, DC. From 1969 to 1992 he was a member of the editorial board of *Concilium*. His latest book is *Sacrament: The Language of God's Giving*, New York 1999.

Address: Catholic University of America, Dept. of Theology, Washington DC 20064, USA

FELIX WILFRED was born in the southernmost district of India in 1948. He is professor in the School of Philosophy and Religious Thought of the State University of Madras, India. Recipient of three gold medals for academic excellence, he pursues study and research in several disciplines in humanities, social sciences, theology, etc. Placing himself at the interstitial space, he is involved in exploring the interconnectedness of academic disciplines and systems in their effort to make sense of the reality. He was also secretary of the Theological Advisory Commission of the Federation of Asian Bishops Conferences and a member of the International Theological Commission. He is a member of the board of directors of *Concilium*. Among his theological publications are: *From the Dusty Soil* (1995), *Beyond Settled Foundations* (1993), *Leave the Temple* (1992), *Sunset in the East?* (1991).

Address: University of Madras, Dept of Christian Studies, Chepauk, Madras, India.

DONNA SINGLES was born in Grand Rapids (Michigan, USA) in 1928.

A doctor in theology, she is a retired member of the teaching staff of the School of Theology of Lyons (The Catholic University of Lyons, France). She has written *Le temps du salut chez saint Irénée*, Lyons 1980; *Et si on ordonnait des femmes?*, Paris 1982; *Des diacres parlent*, Paris 1985; *La gloire de Dieu c'est l'homme vivant*, Paris 1994.

Address: 4 Imp. Catelin, 69002 Lyon, France.

JÜRGEN MOLTMANN was born in Hamburg in 1926 and is a member of the Evangelical Reformed Church of Germany. He studied at Göttingen, and then was Professor at the Kirchliche Hochschule, Wuppertal from 1958 to 1963, Professor of Systematic Theology at the University of Bonn from 1963 to 1967, and until his recent retirement Professor of Systematic Theology in the University of Tübingen. Among his many works are his famous trilogy *Theology of Hope* (1967), *The Crucified God* (1974) and *The Church in the Power of the Spirit* (1992), and his newly completed systematic theology: *The Trinity and the Kingdom of God* (1981), *God in Creation* (1985), *The Way of Jesus Christ* (1989), *The Spirit of Life* (1992) and *The Coming of God* (1996).

Address: Universität Tübingen, Evangelisch-Theologisches Seminar, Liebermeisterstrasse 12, D 72076 Tübingen, Germany.

MARÍA PILAR AQUINO, a Mexican Catholic theologian, is Associate Professor of Theology and Religious Studies and Associate Director of the Center for the Study of Popular Catholicism at the University of San Diego. Her doctoral degree was earned at the Pontifical University of Salamanca, Spain. She has served as President of the Academy of Catholic Hispanic/Latino Theologians of the United States (ACHTUS). She accompanies theologically the experience of US Latina and Latin American communities in academic and pastoral settings. She is the author of *Our Cry for Life. Feminist Theology from Latin America* (New York 1993); *La Teología, La Iglesia y La Mujer en América Latina* (Bogotá, Colombia 1994); the editor of *Aportes para una Teología desde la Mujer* (Madrid 1988), and co-editor of *Theology: Expanding the Borders* (Mystic, CT 1998); *Entre la Indignación y la Esperanza. Teología Feminista Latinoamericana* (Bogotá, Colombia 1998). She has published numerous articles on the feminist experience in the church and in theology.

Address: University of San Diego, Dept of Theology and Religious Studies, 5998 Alcalá Park, San Diego, Ca. 92110–2492, USA.

MARCIANO VIDAL was born in S. Pedro de Trones in the León region of Spain and is a Redemptorist priest. A doctor of theology specializing in morals, he lectures at Comillas Pontifical University in Madrid. He is also director of and professor at the Redemptorists' Higher Institute of Moral Sciences in Madrid. His principal work is the four-volume manual of ethical theology, *Moral de Actitudes* (1995), now in its eighth edition. Recent works include *La familia en la vida y pensamientio de Alfonso de Liguori (1696–1787)* (1995); *Para comprender la objección de conciencia y la insumición* (1995); *Para comprender la Solidaridad: virtud y principio ético* (1996); *La estimativa moral. Propuestas para la educación moral* (1997); *Moral y espiritualidad* (1997).

Address: Manuel Silvela 14, 28010 Madrid, Spain.

EDUARDO DE LA SERNO was born in Buenos Aires, Argentina, in 1955 and ordained priest in 1981. His academic work has been connected with the dialogue between the scriptures and theology, especially liberation theology. He is Professor of Sacred Scripture at the Centre of Philosophical and Theological Studies in the diocese of Quilmes and the Centres of Theological Study of the Salesian and Franciscan fathers in Argentina, as well as teaching at other theological centres for clergy training and at conferences. His books include *Los pies en el Barro, teologia de la misión popular*, Montevideo 1993, and pastoral works on the sects as signs of the times and the cardinal sins. He has also written many articles.

Address: Parroquia Nuestra Señora del Carmen, Corrientes 2040, (1879) Quilmes – Buenos Aires, Argentina.
E-mail: edlserna@wamani.apc.org

J. MATTHEW ASHLEY was born in Gainesville, Florida, USA in 1958. He studied philosophy and physics at St Louis University, theology at the Weston Jesuit School of Theology, and completed a doctorate in Christian Theology from the University of Chicago Divinity School in 1993, with a dissertation on the theology of Johann Baptist Metz. A revision of this work appeared in 1998 as *Interruptions: Mysticism, Politics and Theology in the Work of Johann Baptist Metz*. He is currently an assistant professor of systematic theology at the University of Notre Dame, where he teaches courses on science and religion, fundamental theology, political and liberation theology, and Christian spirituality.

Address: Department of Theology, University of Notre Dame, Notre Dame, Indiana 46556, USA.

JON SOBRINO was born in the Basque Country in 1938 and educated in Spain; Germany, where he gained a doctorate in theology; and the USA, from where, unique among liberation theologians, he holds a master's degree in engineering mechanics. He joined the Society of Jesus in 1956 and has since 1957 belonged to the Central American province and lived mainly in El Salvador. His many works translated into English include *Christology at the Crossroads* (1976); *The True Church and the Poor* (1984); *Jesus in Latin America* (1986); *Spirituality of Liberation* (1988); *Companions of Jesus: The Murder and Martyrdom of the Salvadorean Jesuits* (1990). With the late Ignacio Ellacuría, he is joint editor of *Mysterium Liberationis: Fundamental Concepts of Liberation Theology* (1993). The first volume of his two-volume christology, *Jesus the Liberator*, appeared in 1993, and the second, *Following Jesus Christ*, will be published in 2001.

PEDRO CASALDÁLIGA was born in Spain of Catalan stock in 1928 and is a Claretian missionary. He has lived in Brazil since 1968 and in 1971 was ordained bishop in the Prelacy of São Félix do Araguaia, in the province of Mato Grosso. A poet and writer, he is also vice-president of the Pastoral Land Commission. His works include *Uma Igreja da Amazônia em conflicto com o Latifúndio e a Marginalizacão social* (1971); *Creo na Justiça e na Esperança* (translated into English); *Tierra nuestra, Libertad*. He is also part author of the *Missa da terra sem males* and *Missa dos Quilombos* and, with José-María Virgil, of *The Spirituality of Liberation* (English trans. 1994).

Address: Prelazia de São Félix do Araguaia, CX Postal 05, CEP. 78.670.000 S. Félix do Araguaia MT, Brazil.

The editors wish to thank the following colleagues who contributed in a most helpful way to the final project.

M. Althaus-Reid	Edinburgh	Scotland
J. Argüello	Managua	Nicaragua
G. Baum	Montreal	Canada
V. J. Berkenbrock	Petropolis	Brazil
W. Beuken	Leuven	Belgium
F. Castillo	Santiago	Chile
F. Elizondo	Madrid	Spain
M. Fabri dos Anjos	São Paulo	Brazil
C. Floristán	Madrid	Spain
R. Gibellini	Brescia	Italy
F. Heselaars Hartono	Jakarta	Indonesia
M. E. Hunt	Silver Spring	America
B. Kern	Mainz	Germany
U. King	Bristol	England
H. Laubach	Mainz	Germany
F. Magnis-Suseno	Jakarta	Indonesia
N. Mette	Münster	Germany
J. B. Metz	Münster	Germany
H. Meyer-Wilmes	Nijmegen	The Netherlands
D. N. Power	Washington	America
M. Purwatma	Yogyakarta	Indonesia
G. Ruggieri	Catania	Italy
D. Singles	Lyon	France
P. Suess	São Paulo	Brazil
E. Tamez	San José	Costa Rica
C. Theobald	Paris	France
M. Vidal	Madrid	Spain
F. Wilfred	Madras	India

CONCILIUM

Foundation

A. van den Boogaard	President	Nijmegen	The Netherlands
P. Brand	Secretary	Ankeveen	The Netherlands
H. Häring		Nijmegen	The Netherlands
W. Jeanrond		Lund	Sweden
D. Mieth		Tübingen	Germany
C. Theobald SJ		Paris	France

Founders

A. van den Boogaard	Nijmegen	The Netherlands
P. Brand	Ankeveen	The Netherlands
Y. Congar OP†	Paris	France
H. Küng	Tübingen	Germany
J.-B. Metz	Vienna	Austria
K. Rahner SJ†	Innsbruck	Austria
E. Schillebeeckx OP	Nijmegen	The Netherlands

Directors

Maria Pilar Aquino Vargas	San Diego, CA	USA
José Oscar Beozzo	São Paulo, SP	Brazil
Sean Freyne	Dublin	Ireland
Hermann Häring	Nijmegen	The Netherlands
Maureen Junker-Kenny	Dublin	Ireland
Werner Jeanrond	Lund	Sweden
Karl-Josef Kuschel	Tübingen	Germany
Dietmar Mieth	Tübingen	Germany
Giuseppe Ruggieri	Catania	Italy
Elisabeth Schüssler Fiorenza	Cambridge, MA	USA
Jon Sobrino SJ	San Salvador	El Salvador
Janet Martin Soskice	Cambridge	United Kingdom
Elsa Tamez	San José, CA	Costa Rica
Christoph Theobald SJ	Paris	France
Miklós Tomka	Budapest	Hungary
David Tracy	Chicago, IL	USA
Marciano Vidal CssR	Madrid	Spain
Felix Wilfred	Madras	India
Ellen van Wolde	Tilburg	The Netherlands

General Secretariat: Prins Bernhardstraat 2, 6521 AB Nijmegen, The Netherlands
Manager: Mrs E. C. Duindam-Deckers